Contents

General editor: Graham Handley MA PhD

Brodie's Notes on Chaucer's

The Wife of Bath's Tale

I. G. Handyside MA
Formerly Kingswood School, Bath

Revised by P. Gooden BA
Kingswood School, Bath

Pan Books London and Sydney

This revised edition published 1987 by
Pan Books Ltd, Cavaye Place, London SW10 9PG
9 8 7 6 5 4 3 2

Revised by P. Gooden 1987
ISBN 0 330 50243 3
Photoset by Parker Typesetting Service, Leicester
Printed and bound in Great Britain by
Richard Clay Ltd, Bungay, Suffolk

Preface

This student revision aid is based on the principle that any close examination of Chaucer's text is essential to a full understanding of his artistry. He is by common agreement one of our greatest comic poets, and *The Canterbury Tales* is his masterpiece. But because his language is not easy to understand, some due attention must be given to it and the ways in which it differs from our language today. Consequently each editor of a parallel text Chaucer in this series will give an account of Chaucer's grammar, versification and pronunciation.

The full text of the *Tale* will be given on the left hand side of the page, and opposite this there will be a colloquial prose translation. This must not be regarded as a 'crib'. Students should read it carefully against the original, consulting the glossary and textual notes in order to arrive at a full understanding of the meaning and, one hopes, of the nature of Chaucer's art. That art will be examined by each editor, who will deal with Chaucer's characterization, his humour, his narrative skills, the images he uses, indeed any aspect of his work which merits critical attention and comment. And further, when one has learned to read Chaucer and appreciate him, some knowledge will be necessary of the age in which he lived, and his place in it if that appreciation is to be extended. There will be a brief account of Chaucer's life and times, and the student is advised to look carefully at the textual notes and the critical commentary mentioned above. Revision questions and general questions are also included, and there will be a guideline note-form answer to one of the questions. The aim is not merely to prepare the student thoroughly for an examination, but also to introduce him to the challenge and delight of Chaucer by involving him directly with the text. That text is its own reward, for both the *Prologue* and the *Tales* are among the greatest imaginative literature of all time.

Graham Handley

Literary terms used in these notes

ambivalence Existence within an individual of different or contradictory feelings towards the same object. The Wife of Bath is ambivalent in her attitude towards marriage: it is the source of both tribulation and delight.

irony Easier to detect in practice than to define. The term 'ironic' can be applied to the gap between the way things look and the way they really are; it can describe a sudden and unexpected reversal of events in a story; it can be used of a phrase, even a word, whose 'real' meaning (intended to be so interpreted by reader or listener) is somehow at odds with the 'dictionary' meaning. Respective examples of the above from *The Wife of Bath's Prologue and Tale* are: the tremendous denunciation made by the Wife of her first three husbands, in which she accuses them of offences which she has herself committed. In the *Tale*, the way in which the knight escapes from a sentence of death only to fall victim to what he regards as being a fate just as dreadful – marriage to the old woman – is an example of an ironic turn of events. When the Wife describes her first husbands as 'goode men, and riche, and olde', the word 'goode' has an ironic dimension: they were 'good' for the Wife in that they were likely to die soon and leave her their money, also in that they were submissive to her during their lives. However, in her attacks on them, she suggests that they were the very opposite of 'good' (i.e. virtuous). The above categories and examples of irony give only a very limited idea of its scope.

A brief description of Chaucer's life and works

Geoffrey Chaucer was born about 1340 near the Tower of London. He was born into the age of Edward III, and of the Black Prince, into the Age of Chivalry and the magnificent court of Edward III with knights and ladies, heraldry and tournaments, minstrels and poetry, music and story-telling.

Chaucer entered into this rich and colourful courtly world at an early age, when he became a page in the household of the Countess of Ulster, wife to Lionel, later Duke of Clarence, and one of the sons of Edward III. This was clearly arranged by his parents, who had some contacts at Court. His mother's first husband had been Keeper of the King's Wardrobe, and there can be little doubt that she had something to do with the appointment of Chaucer's father as deputy to the King's Butler. The first record of Geoffrey Chaucer appears in an account book, dating from 1357, which records a payment by the royal household to a London tailor for a cloak, multi-coloured breeches and a pair of shoes for the young page Chaucer. It was in the Duke's great houses in London and Yorkshire that the young page would have learned the elegant and aristocratic code of manners, and made the acquaintance of the high and the noble. He would have learned French and Latin, the languages of the Court, the Church and the educated classes. It was also one of the duties of a page to play and sing, and to recite poetry.

The next record we have is that Chaucer was taken prisoner by the French in 1359, during one of the campaigns in The Hundred Years' War, and ransomed in the following year – the King himself contributing £16 (a very large sum in those days) of the money. So Chaucer must have seen active service in the French wars, probably as a squire attending on one of the nobles, like the squire in the *Canterbury Tales* who attended on the Knight, his father. For the upper classes, the experience of being a prisoner of war in the Age of Chivalry was not too uncomfortable. It was normal for the 'prisoner' to be entertained as a 'house guest' until the ransom was paid, and it is probable that during this enforced stay in France Chaucer became thoroughly versed in French literature, particularly the *Roman de la Rose* (the procedure manual, as it were, for 'courtly love'), which was to have such an important influence on his literary work.

After his ransom was paid, Chaucer returned to his Court duties, and was soon in a more elevated position. He became one of the valets in attendance on the King. In 1366 his father died and his mother married again. It is probable that in the same year he married Philippa, daughter of Sir Payne Roet and sister of Katherine Swynford, the mistress and later third wife to John of Gaunt. Philippa was a lady-in-waiting to the Queen. As a valet to the King, Chaucer would carry candles 'before the King', tidy up his bedroom and attend to a variety of duties which were to become more and more concerned with affairs of state. In 1386 he was sent abroad on the official business of the Crown. About this time he was promoted from valet to palace official. It appears that Chaucer went soldiering again in 1369, probably on one of John of Gaunt's campaigns in Picardy. In 1370 he was abroad again on the King's service, and we can now see him becoming a trusted civil servant as he was frequently sent on missions to France, Flanders and Italy. During his visits to Italy on official business Chaucer took the opportunity to become familiar with Italian literature, most especially the works of Petrarch, Boccaccio and Dante, which were to influence much of his subsequent poetry.

In 1374 he was promoted to a senior position as Comptroller of Customs and Subsidy (for wool, skins and hides) at the Port of London, and the City of London bestowed on him the lease of a house in Aldgate.

From about 1380 Chaucer settled down to his life as senior customs official, as there is only one record of further journeys abroad. He must have been respected as a man of affairs, as he became a Justice of the Peace in 1385, and a Member of Parliament, or Knight of the Shire for Kent, soon afterwards.

It was during these years that Chaucer found time to write seriously. His early literary attempts were influenced considerably by French literature. Then, when John of Gaunt left the country in 1386 on an adventure to claim the crown of Castile, the King's uncle, the Duke of Gloucester, took charge of the country's affairs (Richard being not yet of age), and Chaucer suffered from the new influences in royal patronage. He lost his

Comptrollership of Customs, he was not re-elected to Parliament and he had to give up his house in Aldgate. We even learn that he felt himself in danger of being sued for debt. Chaucer had now plenty of time to ponder and at this time he must have been preparing *The Canterbury Tales.*

In 1389 a rumour was abroad that the great Duke of Lancaster (Chaucer's patron John of Gaunt) was returning home. This helped the young King Richard II in taking over the reins of power from his uncle Gloucester. It has been stated that the young King Richard knew Chaucer and liked his poetry. There must be some substance in this, as shortly afterwards Chaucer was appointed Clerk of the King's Works. John of Gaunt returned to England in November 1389, and for the rest of his life Chaucer was to enjoy royal patronage and a comfortable living. It was in these years of semi-retirement that *The Canterbury Tales* were written. Alas, Chaucer died without having finished his masterpiece. His tomb in Westminster Abbey gives the date of his death – October 1400.

It seems probable that 1387 was the approximate date of commencement for *The Canterbury Tales.* Chaucer's renown rests mainly on this work, but in terms of volume the *Tales* form less than half of his writing which has come down to us. Besides a number of shorter poems, there are five other major works in verse and two or three in prose. Chaucer's most important production during his first tentative years as a writer was the translation he probably made of the *Roman de la Rose*, the style and content of which were to have such a great influence on his writing. His first major poem was *The Book of the Duchess*, a poem steeped in the French tradition, written about 1370 to commemorate the death of Blanche, Duchess of Lancaster and wife of his patron, John of Gaunt. This was the first of four love-vision poems, the others being *The House of Fame*, *The Parliament of Fowls* and *The Legend of Good Women* (whose date is doubtful). Chaucer's works can be conveniently grouped into three parts, the French period, the Italian period and the English period; and, generally speaking, the periods follow one another in chronological sequence. The French period showed the influence of the *Roman de la Rose*, and included the love-vision poems. The Italian period (1380–5), is marked by the narrative poem *Troilus and Criseyde*, which rehandles a theme of the Italian poet Boccaccio. *Troilus and Criseyde* is a masterpiece, and is still considered to be the finest narrative poem in English, full of beauty and lyrical quality, and delightful humour in the character of Pandarus. The English period (1389–1400) is the last, and is the period when Chaucer reached his full maturity as a dramatic poet. This is the period of *The Canterbury Tales*, a collection of tales and tellers which is unique in English literature. Chaucer died before he could complete this great masterpiece.

It must be emphasized that these terms, 'French,' 'Italian', 'English' for Chaucer's literary life only indicate predominant influences: the stories in *The Canterbury Tales* are drawn from far and wide; *The Knight's Tale*, for instance, again owes its theme to a story by Boccaccio.

Setting and plot of the *Tale*

Setting

The Wife of Bath's Tale is but one of a collection of stories and introductions to the stories that make up *The Canterbury Tales*. *The Tales* is unquestionably Chaucer's great masterpiece, his most ambitious and comprehensive work, and his last. The individual tales were composed at various times during Chaucer's literary career and brought together, with others specially written for the purpose, as a collection of stories told within the framework of a pilgrimage to Canterbury. There are many examples in the literature of the Middle Ages of collections of stories, or 'novelle', and there is no doubt that Chaucer was familiar with some of them. Nevertheless, whatever the examples, *The Canterbury Tales* is unique. By choosing a pilgrimage as the frame-story within which to tell his tales, Chaucer, in a brilliant stroke of genius, was able to bring together, as pilgrims, a representative group of various classes of English society of his time, and to allocate to each pilgrim a tale suited to character and status.

Chaucer's ambitious plan for *The Canterbury Tales* was never completed. In the *General Prologue* we are told that each pilgrim will tell four tales, two on the outward and another two on the homeward journey. But the company never reaches Canterbury and there are manuscripts of tales for only twenty-three of the thirty pilgrims, and these incompletely arranged. Even so the partly finished work is the great masterpiece of comic poetry in English literature.

The dramatic coherence of *The Canterbury Tales* is fashioned by the *General Prologue* which sets the scene of the pilgrimage to Canterbury, and introduces the pilgrims by a striking series of word portraits. These portraits of the pilgrims leap out of the pages with all the vividness of description and character of great portrait painting, and with astounding originality and realism. As Nevill Coghill comments: 'The result was a new sort of poetical truth, the creation of a poetry of fact by a wise, sure-eyed and sensitive selection of daily detail, mellowed and harmonized by a humane and often an amused approval, qualified whenever approval was withdrawn by an ironical wit. It was a new way of looking at people.' So diverse are the characters and so vivid the portraiture, that the *General Prologue* has been described as The National Portrait Gallery of Medieval England; the portraits of a nation, of 'high and low, old and young, male and female, lay and clerical, learned and ignorant, rogue and righteous, land and sea, town and country.' The portrait of the Wife of Bath from the *General Prologue* is included before the text of the *Wife of Bath's Prologue* and *Tale*. She is described as a hearty provincial middle-aged woman, partially deaf, with a bold and ruddy face and a gap in her teeth; of full figure, wearing gaudy stockings and an outsized hat. By all accounts she was a first-class cloth-maker, with a penchant for fine clothes (though a little out-of-date) and for giving advice in matters of the heart; somewhat domineering and of some local importance; a chatterbox with an obsession for husbands, travel and company.

The portrait of the Wife of Bath is included because it is an essential part of the Wife's *Prologue*, and in some respects of the tale itself. In keeping with the diversity of characters is the wide range of stories which are assigned to the pilgrims, each tale being suited to the character and vocation of the teller. Almost every type of medieval fiction and literary form is represented in the collection of tales – the romance of chivalry, the courtly lay, the beast-epic, the legend or Saint's life, the sermon and moral discourse, and the coarse realistic 'fabliaux', which were the vulgar and scurrilous stories of the lower social classes. The *Wife of Bath's Tale* and its *Prologue* are unusual in the context of the other prologues and their tales. Normally the prologues, or links, are short and act as dramatic interludes between the tales, adding drama and giving movement and reality to the frame-story. The *Prologue* here is very different, in that *The Wife*'s *Prologue* is her main contribution (in length as long as the *General Prologue*), with her tale as a subsidiary element – a sort of 'exemplum' for her 'sermon' on marriage. The dramatic link, the usual reason for the prologues, is to be found at the very end of the *The Wife*'s Prologue, with the quarrel between the Friar and the Summoner leading naturally into the tale itself. This *Prologue* is unique: an extraordinary autobiographical 'tour de force' in the tradition of the scholastic philosophical 'argumentum'; and her tale a folklore story of romance, tailored to suit the conclusions of her argument.

In the *General Prologue* to *The Canterbury Tales* we learn that Chaucer had already taken up his quarters at the Tabard Inn, Southwark, in preparation for his pilgrimage to Canterbury the next day, when twenty-nine other people arrive at the Inn for the same purpose. The landlord of the Tabard Inn, the 'Host' Harry Bailly, learning the purpose of the assembled company, proposes that the pilgrims should entertain themselves during the journey by telling one another stories. The company accepts this suggestion and, when the host announces his intention of joining the party on the pilgrimage, decides to appoint him as organizer and judge of the tales. There would be a prize for the best tale told – a good supper at the Tabard Inn, at the expense of the other companions, on their return. Certain matters of discipline are also discussed and all the company agree to abide by the rules laid down by the host, any breach of which would involve a fine amounting to the travelling expenses of the whole company. The company starts off on the journey to Canterbury early next morning; it is decided by lot that the Knight, the most distinguished member of the party, shall tell the first tale. And so the sequence of story-telling begins.

Plot

What the Wife of Bath says is split into *Prologue* and *Tale*. The *Prologue* is a mixture of argument and autobiography, the first autobiography in English fiction, it has been claimed. She begins with some generalized comment in favour of marriage(s) and then, after almost 200 lines, turns to a chronological account of her varied relationships with five husbands. This 'long preamble', as the Friar calls it, is followed by a story which is scarcely half the length of its 'introduction'. The action of the *Tale* can be summarized as follows:

A knight of King Arthur's household rapes a young woman, for which crime he is condemned to death. The queen and other ladies of the court intercede on the knight's behalf and he is delivered up to them so that they can decide his fate. They offer to spare his life if he can provide the answer to the question, 'What is it that women most desire?'. He is given a year and a day to produce a satisfactory solution but, despite a widespread search, is unable to find any two people who will agree on what it is that women most want. Returning home, his quest a failure, he encounters a very ugly old woman who promises him an answer if he, in turn, will consent to any demand she might make of him. The knight agrees to the bargain, the hag whispers the information in his ear, and the man later delivers this 'secret' to the assembled court of women: it is that women wish most of all to have the upper hand over husband or lover. No-one contradicts the knight's conclusion, but at this point the hag claims her reward – he must now marry her. The knight is horrified but has no choice. On the wedding-night the old woman defends herself against his accusations that she is ugly, old and of low breeding. Finally she offers him the choice: he can have her either old, ugly and faithful or young, beautiful and probably unfaithful. The knight cannot choose between these tricky alternatives and leaves the decision to his old bride. This surrender of authority is what she requires and, as a prize, she claims that she will be both beautiful *and* virtuous. She undergoes a magical transformation and the delighted knight discovers that he has a fair young wife who promises him fidelity. They live happily ever after.

The Wife of Bath's Tale in Chaucer's Middle English, with a translation into modern English

The portrait of the Wife of Bath

(from the General Prologue, lines 445–76)

A good Wyf was ther of bisyde Bathe,
But she was som-del deef and that was scathe.
Of clooth-makýng she hadde swich an haunt
She passed hem of Ypres and of Gaunt.
In al the parisshe wyf ne was ther noon
That to the offrýnge bifore hire sholde goon,
And if ther dide, certeyn so wrooth was she,
That she was out of alle charitee.
Hir coverchiefs ful fyne were of ground:
I dorste swere they weyeden ten pound,
That on a Sonday were upon hir heed.
Hir hosen weren of fyn scarlet reed
Ful streite y-teyd, and shoes ful moyste and newe;
Boold was hir face and fair and reed of hewe.

She was a worthy womman al hir lyve;
Housbondes at chirche dore she hadde fyve,
Withouten oother companye in youthe,
But ther-of nedeth nat to speke as nowthe:
And thrýdes hádde she béen at Jérusalém;
She hadde passed many a straunge strem;
At Rome she hadde been and at Boloigne,
In Galice at Seint Jame, and at Coloigne;
She coude muchel of wandrynge by the weye:
Gat-tothed was she, soothly for to seye.

Upon an amblere esily she sat,
Y-wympled wel, and on hir heed an hat
As brood as is a bokeler or a targe;
A foot-mantel aboute hir hipes large,
And on his feet a paire of spores sharpe.
In felawshipe wel coude she laughe and carpe;
Of remedyes of love she knew perchaunce,
For she coude of that art the olde daunce.

The portrait of the Wife of Bath

(from the General Prologue, lines 445–76)

A good Wife was there from the neighbourhood of Bath. She was somewhat deaf, and that was a pity. She had such skill in cloth-making that she surpassed the work of the cloth-makers of Ypres and Ghent. In all her parish there was no woman who went in front of her when the offerings were made, and if one did, then she was certainly so angry that she was put out of all charity. Her head coverings were of the finest texture; I dare say that the ones she wore on her head on Sundays must have weighed ten pounds. Her hose were of fine red scarlet, laced tightly around, and her shoes were soft and new. Bold was her face, handsome and ruddy in complexion.

She had been a woman of some importance all her life; she had married five husbands at the church door, apart from other company in her youth – but there is no need to say anything more about that: and three times she had been to Jerusalem; she had passed over many a foreign river; she had even been at Rome and at Boulogne, in Galicia at the shrine of Saint James, and at Cologne; she really knew a lot about wandering by the way: she was gap-toothed, to tell the truth.

She sat with ease on an ambling horse, well wimpled, and on her head a hat as broad as a buckler or a shield; she had a saddle-rug around her large hips, and on her feet a pair of sharp spurs. In company she could enjoy herself and chatter; and as it happened she understood a lot about the remedies of love, for she knew everything about the old tricks on that subject.

The Wife of Bath's Prologue

Experience, though noon auctoritee
Were in this world, is right ynogh for me
To speke of wo that is in mariage;
For, lordinges, sith I twelve yeer was of age,
Thonked be God that is eterne on live,
Housbondes at chirche dore I have had five –
If I so ofte mighte have ywedded bee –
And alle were worthy men in hir degree.
But me was toold, certeyn, nat longe agoon is,
That sith that Crist ne wente nevere but onis
To wedding, in the Cane of Galilee,
That by the same ensample taughte he me
That I ne sholde wedded be but ones.

Herkne eek, lo, which a sharp word for the nones,
Biside a welle, Jhesus, God and man,
Spak in repreeve of the Samaritan:
'Thou hast yhad five housbondes,' quod he,
'And that ilke man that now hath thee
Is noght thyn housbonde,' thus seyde he certeyn.
What that he mente therby, I kan nat seyn;
But that I axe, why that the fifthe man
Was noon housebonde to the Samaritan?
How manye mighte she have in mariage?
Yet herde I nevere tellen in myn age
Upon this nombre diffinicioun.

Men may devine and glosen, up and doun,
But wel I woot, expres, withoute lie,
God bad us for to wexe and multiplie;
That gentil text kan I wel understonde.
Eek wel I woot, he seyde myn housbonde
Sholde lete fader and mooder, and take to me.
But of no nombre mencion made he,
Of bigamie, or of octogamie;
Why sholde men thanne speke of it vileynie?
    Lo, heere, the wise king, daun Salomon;
I trowe he hadde wives mo than oon.

The Wife of Bath's Prologue

Experience, even if there were no other authority in this world, would be quite enough for me to talk about the unhappiness that is in marriage. For, my Lords, since I was but twelve years old, thanks be to God who is ever eternal, I have had five husbands at the church door – if I might be considered to have been properly married so many times – and all were respectable men of their class. But I was told in no uncertain way, not long ago, that since Christ only went but once to a wedding, in Cana of Galilee, by that same example he taught me that I should not be married more than once.

Consider also what sharp words Jesus, God and man, spoke on that occasion beside a well to rebuke the Samaritan: 'Thou hast had five husbands,' he said, 'and that same man whom thou now hast is not thy husband,' that is what he said, without any doubt. What he meant by it, I cannot say. But this I do ask, why was the fifth man no husband to the Samaritan woman? How many was she allowed to have in marriage? Never yet in my life have I heard a statement made as to the precise number.

People may guess and try to interpret the texts in all sorts of ways, but I really know, without a lie, that God bade us expressly to wax and multiply. That sensible text I well can understand. And also I know well that he said that my husband should leave his father and mother and take me. But he made no mention of any number, or concerning bigamy or octogamy; why then should man speak badly of such things?

And hear this, how about Lord Solomon, the wise king; I believe that he had more wives than just one!

As wolde God it were leveful unto me
To be refresshed half so ofte as he!
Which yifte of God hadde he for alle his wives!
No man hath swich that in this world alive is.
God woot, this noble king, as to my wit,
The firste night had many a mirie fit
With ech of hem, so wel was him on live.
Yblessed be God that I have wedded five!
Welcome the sixte, whan that evere he shal.
For sothe, I wol nat kepe me chaast in al.
When myn housbonde is fro the world ygon,
Som Cristen man shal wedde me anon,
For thanne, th'apostle seith that I am free
To wedde, a Goddes half, where it liketh me.

He seith that to be wedded in no sinne;
Bet is to be wedded than to brinne.
What rekketh me, thogh folk seye vileynie
Of shrewed Lameth and his bigamie?
I woot wel Abraham was an hooly man,
And Jacob eek, as ferforth as I kan;
And ech of hem hadde wives mo than two,
And many another holy man also.
Wher can ye seye, in any manere age,
That hye God defended mariage
By expres word? I pray yow, telleth me.
Or where comanded he virginitee?
I woot as wel as ye, it is no drede,
Th'apostel, whan he speketh of maidenhede,
He seyde that precept therof hadde he noon.

Men may conseille a womman to been oon,
But conseilling is no comandement.
He putte it in oure owene juggement;
For hadde God comanded maidenhede,
Thanne hadde he dampned wedding with the dede.
And certes, if ther were no seed ysowe,
Virginitee, thanne wherof sholde it growe?
Poul dorste nat comanden, atte leeste,
A thing of which his maister yaf noon heeste.
The dart is set up for virginitee:
Cacche whoso may, who renneth best lat see.

Would to God that it had been possible for me to have been refreshed half so often as he! What a gift from God he had with all his wives. No man who is still alive in this world has such an arrangement. God knows, anyway from my point of view, this noble king must have had a merry time with each of them on the first night – luck was with him during his life. Blessed be to God that I have wedded five! Welcome the sixth, whenever he comes along. For in truth, I do not intend to keep myself chaste in any way. When my husband has passed away from this world, some Christian man will wed me again soon enough; for then, the apostle says, on God's behalf, I am free to marry again when it pleases me.

He states that it is no sin to be married – in fact, better to be married than to burn. What do I care if people speak ill of wicked Lamech and his bigamy? I know very well that Abraham was a holy man, and Jacob as well, as far as I know; and each of them had more than two wives, and many another holy man as well. Where can you find evidence, from any period in time, that God on High has expressly prohibited marriage. I pray you, tell me. Or where did he command virginity? I know as well as you do, there is no question about it, that the apostle, when he spoke of maidenhood admitted that he had no authority to command it.

One may advise a woman to be one of those, but advising is not the same as ordering. He left the matter to our own judgement. For if God had commanded maidenhood to all, then by that action he would have condemned marriage: and clearly if the seed were never sown, then where would virginity grow from? Paul did not dare, even in the slightest way, to command something for which his master gave no direction. The prize of the spear is offered for virginity – catch it who can, and let us see who runs the best race!

But this word is nat taken of every wight,
But ther as God lust give it of his might.
I woot wel that th'apostel was a maide;
But nathelees, thogh that he wroot and saide
He wolde that every wight were swich as he,
Al nis but conseil to virginitee.
And for to been a wyf he yaf me leve
Of indulgence; so nis it no repreve
To wedde me, if that my make die,
Withouten excepcion of bigamie.
Al were it good no womman for to touche, –
He mente as in his bed or in his couche;
For peril is bothe fyr and tow t'assemble:
Ye knowe what this ensample may resemble.

This is al and som, he heeld virginitee
Moore parfit than wedding freletee.
Freletee clepe I, but if that he and she
Wolde leden al hir lyf in chastitee.
I graunte it wel, I have noon envie,
Thogh maidenhede preferre bigamie.
It liketh hem to be clene, body and goost;
Of myn estaat I nil nat make no boost.
For wel ye knowe, a lord in his houshold,
He nath nat every vessel al of gold;
Somme been of tree, and doon hir lord servise.
God clepeth folk to hym in sondry wise,
And everich hath of God a propre yifte,
Som this, som that, as him liketh shifte.

Virginitee is greet perfeccion,
And continence eek with devocion,
But Crist, that of perfeccion is welle,
Bad nat every wight he sholde go selle
Al that he hadde, and give it to the poore
And in swich wise folwe him and his foore.
He spak to him that wolde live parfitly;
And lordinges, by youre leve, that am nat I.
I wol bistowe the flour of al myn age
In the actes and in fruit of mariage.

But this recommendation does not apply to everyone, but only where it pleases God to bestow it, in his mightiness. I know very well that the apostle was a virgin; but nevertheless, although he wrote and said that he would rather that everyone were such as he, all this is nothing more than a recommendation in favour of virginity. As a concession, he gave me leave to be a wife, so there is no shame involved in marrying me, if my mate were to die, except of course, in the case of bigamy. Although it may be a good thing not to touch a woman – he meant in bed or on a couch, for it is dangerous to bring together fire and flax – you know very well what that allusion means.

This is the sum and total of what he said, he held virginity to be more perfect than marrying because the flesh is weak. Fraility I call it, except if he and she intend to lead all their lives in chastity.

I grant it freely, I have no envy although virginity is preferred to bigamy. It pleases some to be pure in body and soul; regarding my own position I shall make no such boast. You all know very well that a lord does not have every vessel in his household made out of gold – some are of wood and give just as good service to their lord. God calls his people to Him in many ways, and each one has his special gift from God – some this, some that, as it pleases Him to provide.

Virginity is indeed great perfection, and continence too when followed with devotion. But Christ, who is the source of all perfection, did not command that every person should go and sell all that he had, and give it to the poor, and in that way follow in his footsteps. He addressed himself to those who wanted to live in perfection; and by your leave my lords, I am not one of them. I will bestow the flower of my life in the acts and fruits of marriage.

Telle me also, to what conclusion
Were membres maad of generacion,
And of so parfit wys a wight ywroght?
Trusteth right wel, they were nat maad for noght.
Glose whoso wole, and seye bothe up and doun,
That they were maked for purgacioun
Of urine, and oure bothe thinges smale
Were eek to knowe a femele from a male,
And for noon oother cause, – say ye no?
The experience woot wel it is noght so.
So that the clerkes be nat with me wrothe,
I sey this, that they maked ben for bothe,
This is to seye, for office, and for ese
Of engendrure, ther we nat God displese.

Why sholde men elles in hir bookes sette
That man shal yelde to his wyf hire dette?
Now wherwith sholde he made his paiement,
If he ne used his sely instrument?
Thanne were they maad upon a creature
To purge urine, and eek for engendrure.
But I seye noght that every wight is holde,
That hath swich harneys as I to yow tolde,
To goon and usen hem in engendrure.
Thanne sholde men take of chastitee no cure.
Christ was a maide, and shapen as a man,
And many a seint, sith that the world bigan;
Yet lived they evere in parfit chastitee.
I nil envye no virginitee.

Lat hem be breed of pured whete-seed,
And lat us wifes hoten barly-breed;
And yet with barly-breed, Mark telle kan,
Oure Lord Jhesu refresshed many a man.
In swich estaat as God hath cleped us
I wol persevere; I nam nat precius.
In wyfhood I wol use myn instrument
As frely as my Makere hath it sent.
If I be daungerous, God yeve me sorwe!
Myn housbonde shal it have bothe eve and morwe,
Whan that him list come forth and paye his dette.

Tell me also, to what purpose were the reproductive organs made, and why in such a way is the body fashioned so excellently? Take my word for it, these parts were not made for nothing. Interpret it as you will and argue it anyway you want that they were fashioned merely for the purgation of urine, and that both our little thingamebobs were only put there to distinguish a female from a male, and for no other reason at all – do you say no? Experience knows well that it is not so. In order that the clerics will not be angry with me I declare this, that they were made for both purposes; that is to say, for practical use and for the delights of intercourse, in such ways as we do not displease God.

Why else should men set down in their books that man shall yield his wife her debt? Now in what other way is he to make his payment unless he uses his simple little instrument? It therefore follows that they were created on the body not only to purge urine but also for intercourse.

But I do not imply that everyone who has such equipment as I have just mentioned to you is obliged to go and use it for intercourse. If so, we would show too little respect for chastity. Christ, who was fashioned as a man, was a virgin, and many a saint too, since the world began; and yet they lived always in perfect chastity. I will in no way speak ill of virginity.

Let them be the white bread of purest wheat, and let us wives be known as barley bread; and yet, with barley bread, as Mark could tell us, Our Lord Jesus refreshed many a man. In such estate as God has called us to, I will persevere; I am not too precious, as a wife, I will use my instrument as freely as my Maker gave it. If I should grudge it in any way, God give me sorrow! My husband shall have use of it both evening and morning, in fact, whenever he wants to come along and pay his debt.

An housbonde I wol have, I wol nat lette,
Which shal be bothe my dettour and my thral,
And have his tribulacion withal
Upon his flessh, whil that I am his wyf.
I have the power duringe al my lyf
Upon his propre body, and noghte he.
Right thus the Apostel tolde it unto me;
And bad oure housbondes for to love us weel.
Al this sentence me liketh every deel.
Up stirte the Pardoner, and that anon:
'Now, dame,' quod he, 'by God and by Seint John!
Ye been a noble prechour in this cas.
I was aboute to wedde a wyf; allas,
What sholde I bye it on my flessh so deere?
Yet hadde I levere wedde no wyf to-yeere!'

'Abide!' quod she, 'my tale is nat bigonne.
Nay, thou shalt drinken of another tonne,
Er that I go, shal savoure wors than ale,
And whan that I have toold thee forth my tale
Of tribulacion in mariage,
Of which I am expert in al myn age –
This is to seyn, myself have been the whippe –
Than maystow chese wheither thou wolt sippe
Of thilke tonne that I shal abroche.
Be war of it, er thou to ny approche;
For I shal telle ensamples mo than ten.
"Whoso that nil be war by othere men,
By him shul othere men corrected be."
The same wordes writeth Ptholomee;
Rede in his Almageste, and take it there.'

'Dame, I wolde praye yow, if youre wil it were,'
Seyde this Pardoner, 'as ye bigan,
Telle forth youre tale, spareth for no man,
And teche us younge men of your praktike.'
'Gladly,' quod she, 'sith it may yow like;
But that I praye to al this compaignie,
If that I speke after my fantasie,
As taketh not agrief of that I seye;
For myn entente is nat but for to pleye,
Now, sire, now wol I telle forth my tale.

A husband will I have, I will not be frustrated, who shall be both my debtor and my slave, and suffer the tribulations of the flesh as well, while I am his wife. All through my life I'll have the power over his own body, and not he. Just as the Apostle has told me to; and he commanded our husbands to love us dearly. This is an opinion that pleases me in every way.

At this the Pardoner suddenly started up. 'Now, Madam', he said, 'by God and by Saint John, you are a noble preacher on this subject. I was about to wed a wife, but alas, why should I bring this on myself at such a high price? Now I would rather not marry this year at all.'

'Just wait,' she said, 'my tale is not yet started. Nay, you will drink from another barrel before I am through, and this one will taste worse than ale. And when I have proceeded to tell you my tale of the tribulation of marriage, about which I have been an expert all my life – that is to say, I myself have held the whiphand – then you may choose whether you wish to sip more from this same cask which I shall broach. Be wary of it, ere you come too close, for I shall give you more than ten samples. "Whosoever will not be warned by other men, by other men shall they suffer correction." These same words were written by Ptolemy; read them in his Almagest, you will find it all there.'

'Madam, I pray you, if you would be so kind,' this Pardoner went on, 'proceed to tell your tale as you began: spare nothing because of any man, and teach us young men from your own practical experience.'

'Gladly,' she said, 'since it may please you, but I pray to all this company that if I should speak according to my own belief, you will not take amiss what I say; for my intention is only to amuse you. Now, Sirs, I will get on and tell my tale.'

As evere moote I drinken wyn or ale,
I shal seye sooth, tho housbondes that I hadde,
As thre of him were goode, and two were badde.
The thre were goode men, and riche, and olde;
Unnethe mighte they the statut holde
In which that they were bounden unto me.
Ye woot wel what I meene of this, pardee.
As help me God, I laughe whan I thinke
How pitously a-nigh I made hem swinke!
And, by my fey, I tolde of it no stoor.
They had me yeven hir lond and hir tresoor;
Me neded nat do lenger diligence
To winne hir love, or doon hem reverence.
They loved me so wel, by God above,
That I ne tolde no deyntee of hir love.

A wys womman wol bisie hire evere in oon
To gete hir love, ye, ther as she hath noon.
But sith I hadde hem hoolly in myn hond,
And sith they hadde me yeven al hir lond,
What sholde I taken keep hem for to plese,
But it were for my profit and myn ese?
I sette hem so a-werke, by my fey,
That many a night they songen 'weilawey!'
The bacon was nat fet for him, I trowe,
That som men han in Essex at Dunmowe.
I governed hem so wel, after my lawe,
That ech of hem ful blisful was and fawe
To bringe me gaye thinges fro the faire.
They were ful glad whan I spak to hem faire;
For, God it woot, I chidde hem spitously.

Nor herkneth hou I baar me properly,
Ye wise wives, than kan understonde.
Thus shulde ye speke and bere hem wrong on honde;
For half so boldely kan ther no man
Swere and lyen, as a womman kan.
I sey nat this by wives that been wise,
But if it be whan they hem misavise
A wys wyf shal, if that she can hir good,
Bere him on honde that the cow is wood,
And take witnesse of hir owene maide
Of hir assent; but herkneth how I saide:

As I ever hope to drink wine and ale, I will tell the truth about those husbands that I have had, of the three of them who were good, and the two who were bad. The three who were good men were rich and old; with difficulty could they keep the obligation by which they were bound to me – you know quite well what I mean by this, I am sure. So help me God, I laugh when I think how mercilessly I made them toil each night! And, by my faith, I set no store by it. They had already given me their land and their treasure; and, therfore, it was no longer necessary for me to take any trouble to gain their love, or to show them reverence. They loved me so well, by God above, that I did not have to set much value on their affection.

Indeed, a wise woman will always busy herself to acquire this love when she has not got it. But since I had them completely in the palm of my hand and since they had given me all their land, why then should I take any trouble to please them, unless it should be for my own profit and pleasure? I set them so to work, by my faith, that many a night they wailed, 'Have mercy on me!' The side of bacon that some people receive at Dunmow in Essex was never offered to them you may be sure. I managed them so well, in my own way, that each of them was only too happy and keen to bring me nice things from the fair. They were really delighted when I spoke to them pleasantly; for God knows, I did chide them cruelly.

Now listen how prudently I conducted myself, you wise wives who can understand. You should address yourself in such a way as to put them in the wrong; for there is no man who knows how to swear and lie half so boldly as a woman can. I do not say this is the way for wives who are prudent, except only when they have made a mistake. A prudent wife, if she knows what is good for her, will convince her husband that the chough is mad, and call as witness her own maid who was a party to the deceit; but listen how I held forth:

'Sire olde kaynard, is this thyn array?
Why is my neighebores wyf so gay?
She is honoured over al ther she gooth;
I sitte at hoom, I have no thrifty clooth.
What dostow at my neighebores hous?
Is she so fair? artow so amorous?
What rowne ye with oure maide? *Benedicite!*
Sire olde lecchour, lat thy japes be.
And if I have a gossib or a freend,
Withouten gilt, thou chidest as a feend,
If that I walke or pleye unto his hous.
Thou comest hoom as dronken as a mous,
And prechest on thy bench, with ivel preef!
Thou seist to me it was a greet meschief
To wedde a povre womman, for costage;
And if that she be riche, of heigh parage,
Thanne seistow that it is a tormentrie
To soffre hire pride and hire malencolie.

And if that she be fair, thou verray knave,
Thou seist that every holour wol hire have;
She may no while in chastitee abide,
That is assailled upon ech a side.
Thou seist som folk desiren us for richesse,
Somme for oure shap, and somme for oure fairnesse,
And som for she kan outher singe or daunce,
And som for gentilesse and daliaunce;
Som for hir handes and hir armes smale:
Thus goth al to the devel, by thy tale.
Thou seist men may nat kepe a castel wal,
It may so longe assailled been over al.

'And if that she be foul, thou seist that she
Coveiteth every man that she may se,
For as a spaynel she wol on him lepe,
Til that she finde som man hire to chepe.
Ne noon so grey goos gooth ther in the lake
As, sëistow, wol been withoute make.
And seist it is an hard thing for to welde
A thing that no man wole, his thankes, helde.

'Sir, you old dotard, is this the way to treat me? Why is my neighour's wife so smartly dressed? She is honoured above everyone wherever she goes; while I sit at home having no decent clothes to wear. And what were you doing at my neighbour's house? Is she so attractive? And are you so amorous? What are you whispering to our maid? Heaven bless us! Old Sir lecher, leave be with your pranks. And if I should have acquaintance with a relative or a friend in all innocence, you scold me like the devil, if I should walk or stroll towards his house. You come home as drunk as a mouse, and preach at me from your chair, a curse on you! You tell me that it is a great disadvantage to marry a poor woman, as far as expense is concerned; and if she is rich, and of high rank, then you say that it is a nightmare to suffer her pride and her melancholy.

And if she happens to be pretty, you old wretch, you say that every lecher wants to have her; thus she, who is assailed on every side, cannot remain chaste for very long.

'You say that some men desire us for our wealth, some for our body, and some for our good looks; and some others because a woman knows either how to sing or dance; and some want a woman for her softness and love-making; and even some because of her dainty hands and arms; and in this way we all go to the devil, by your account. You say that nobody can keep safe a castle wall when it is being attacked all round for so long.

'And if she is ugly, you then say that she desires every man that she lays eyes on, in order to leap on him like any spaniel, until she finds someone who will give her what she wants; there is no goose, you say, in any lake that is so grey that it cannot find a mate. And you say that it is hard to control something that no man would willingly keep hold of.

Thus seistow, lorel, when thow goost to bedde;
And that no wys man nedeth for to wedde,
Ne no man that entendeth unto hevene.
With wilde thonder-dint and firy levene
Moote thy welked nekke be tobroke!
'Thow seist that dropping houses, and eek smoke,
And chiding wives maken men to flee
Out of hir owene hous; a, *benedicitee!*
What eyleth swich an old man for to chide?
'Thow seist we wives wol oure vices hide
Til we be fast, and thanne we wol hem shewe –
Wel may that be a proverbe of a shrewe!

'Thou seist that oxen, asses, hors, and houndes,
They been assayed at diverse stoundes;
Bacins, lavours, er that men hem bye,
Spoones and stooles, and al swich housbondrie,
And so been pottes, clothes, and array;
But folk of wives maken noon assay,
Til they be wedded; olde dotard shrewe!
And thanne, seistow, we wol oure vices shewe.
'Thou seist also that it displeseth me
But if that thou wolt preyse my beautee,
And but thou poure alwey upon my face,
And clepe me "faire dame" in every place.
And but thou make a feeste on thilke day
That I was born, and make me fressh and gay;
And but thou do to my norice honour,
And to my chamberere withinne my bour,
And to my fadres folk and his allies –
Thus seistow, olde barel-ful of lies!

'And yet of oure apprentice Janekin,
For his crispe here, shininge as gold so fyn,
And for he squiereth me bothe up and doun,
Yet hastow caught a fals suspecioun.
I wol him noght, thogh thou were deed tomorwe!
'But tell me this: why hidestow, with sorwe,
The keyes of thy cheste awey fro me?
It is my good as wel as thyn, pardee!
What, wenestow make an idiot of oure dame?

These things you say, you wretch, when you go up to bed, and that no sensible man needs to marry, at least no man who intends to go to heaven. May wild thunderbolts and fiery lightning flash break your withered old neck!

'You say that leaking houses, and smoke, and nagging wives make men flee out of their own house; heaven preserve us! What ails such an old man to complain so much?

'You say we wives all hide our vices until we are safe and married and then we will let them be seen – that's a good proverb for a churlish old man!

'You say that oxen, asses, horses and hounds that they are tried out at various times; as well as basins and washing bowls, before people buy them; and spoons and stools and all such household things, and so are pots, clothes and furnishings; but people do not put wives to the test until they are married – you critical old fool! And then, you say, we make our vices apparent.

'You say also that I am unhappy unless you praise my beauty, and unless you remark on my features, and address me as "good madam" in every place. And unless you hold a feast on the day on which I was born, and make arrangements for me to look attractive and well-dressed; and unless you treat my nurse courteously, and the chamber-maid in my room, and my father's relatives and associates – all this you say, you old barrelful of lies!

'And even with regard to our apprentice Jankin, because of his curly hair shining like fine gold, and because he escorts me everywhere, you must have got hold of some nasty suspicions. I wouldn't want him at all, even though you were to die tomorrow!

'But tell me this, why do you hide the keys of your money chest from me? – may you be sorry for it! It is my property as well as yours, by God! What, do you want to make a fool of your mistress?

Now by that lord that called is Seint Jame,
Thou shalt nat bothe, thogh that thou were wood,
Be maister of my body and of my good;
That oon thou shalt forgo, maugree thine yen.
What helpith it of me to enquere or spyen?
I trowe thou woldest loke me in thy chiste!
  Thou sholdest seye, "Wyf, go wher thee liste;
Taak youre disport, I wol nat leve no talis.
I knowe yow for a trewe wyf, dame Alis."
We love no man that taketh kep or charge
Wher that we goon; we wol ben at oure large.

  'Of alle men yblessed moot he be,
The wise astrologien, Daun Ptholome,
That seith this proverbe in his Almageste:
"Of alle men his wisdom is the hyeste
That rekketh nevere who hath the world in honde."
By this proverbe thou shalt understonde,
Have thou ynogh, what thar thee recche or care
How mirily that othere folkes fare?
For, certeyn, olde dotard, by youre leve,
Ye shul have queynte right ynogh at eve.
He is to greet a nigard that wolde werne
A man to lighte a candle at his lanterne;
He shal have never the lasse light, pardee.
Have thou ynogh, thee thar nat pleyne thee.

  'Thou seist also, that if we make us gay
With clothing, and with precious array,
That it is peril of oure chastitee;
And yet, with sorwe! thou most enforce thee,
And seye thise wordes in the Apostles name:
"In habit maad with chastitee and shame
Ye wommen shul apparaille yow," quod he,
"And noght in tressed heer and gay perree,
As perles, ne with gold, no clothes riche."
After thy text, ne after thy rubriche,
I wol nat wirche as muchel as a gnat.
  'Thou seydest this, that I was lyk a cat;
For whoso wolde senge a cattes skin,
Thanne wolde the cat wel dwellen in his in;

Now by that noble man who is called St James, you will not be both master of my body and of my property, even though you were fury itself. One of them you will have to forego, in spite of your intention. What good does it do to watch and spy on me? I believe that you would like to lock me up in your chest!

You should say, "Wife, go wherever you want; go and amuse yourself. I will not allow any tales to be told. I know you for a true wife, Dame Alice." We cannot have affection for any man who takes too much trouble or care about where we go; we will have our freedom.

'Above all men may he be blessed, that wise astrologer, Master Ptolemy, who in his Almagest quoted this proverb: "Of all men whose wisdom is the most superior is he that never cares who holds the world in his hands." From this proverb you should understand that if you have enough yourself, why should you concern yourself or worry about how happily other people manage? For, certainly, by your leave you old fool, you should have had quite enough love-making at night. He is too big a niggard who would prevent another man to light a candle in his lantern; he will not have less light for it, by God. If you have enough, then there is no reason for you to complain.

'You also say that if we make ourselves attractive in our dress, and deck ourselves with gleaming accessories, then this will imperil our chastity; and yet, and may you be sorry for it, you must needs re-inforce your argument by quoting the following words in the Apostle's name: "In habit prepared with decorum and modesty you women shall dress yourselves," he said, "and not with elaborate hair styles and bright jewellery as pearls or gold, and not with expensive clothes." Neither according to your text, nor to its instructions will I take as much notice as a fly.

'You also said that I was like a cat; for if someone would only singe a cat's skin, then will the cat stay put at home.

And if the cattes skin be slik and gay,
She wol nat dwelle in house half a day,
But forth she wole, er any day be dawed,
To shewe hir skin, and goon a-caterwawed.
This is to seye, if I be gay, sire shrewe,
I wol renne out, my borel for to shewe.
'Sire olde fool, what helpeth thee to spyen?
Thogh thou preye Argus with his hundred yen
To be my warde-cors, as he kan best,
In feith, he shal nat kepe me but me lest;
Yet koude I make his berd, so moot I thee!
'Thou seydest eek that ther been thinges thre,
The whiche thinges troublen al this erthe,
And that no wight may endure the ferthe.

O leeve sire shrewe, Jhesu shorte thy lyf!
Yet prechestow and seist an hateful wyf
Yrekened is for oon of thise meschances.
Been ther none othere maner resemblances
That ye may likne youre parables to,
But if a sely wyf be oon of tho?
'Thou liknest eek wommenes love to helle,
To bareyne lond, ther water may nat dwelle.
Thou liknest it also to wilde fyr;
The moore it brenneth, the moore it hath desir
To consume every thing that brent wole be.
Thou seyest, right as wormes shende a tree,
Right so a wyf destroyeth hire housbonde;
This knowe they that been to wives bonde.'

Lordinges, right thus, as ye have understonde,
Baar I stifly mine olde housbondes on honde
That thus they seyden in hir dronkenesse;
And al was fals, but that I took witnesse
On Janekin, and on my nece also.
O Lord! the peyne I dide hem and the wo,
Ful giltelees, by Goddes sweete pine!
For as an hors I koude bite and whine.
I koude pleyne, and yit was in the gilt,
Or elles often time hadde I been spilt.
Whoso that first to mille comth, first grint;
I pleyned first, so was oure werre ystint.

And if the cat's skin is sleek and attractive, then she won't stay at home for half a day, but forth she will go, before the day has dawned, to show off her fur and go a-caterwauling. Which is to say, you old scold, that if I am nicely dressed, I will run out and show off my clothes.

'You old fool, what use is it for you to spy on me? Even though you beg that Argus with his hundred eyes should be my bodyguard, as he knows best how to, in faith, he could not guard me safely unless I allowed him to; I could still outwit him, you can be sure!

'You said also that there are three things which are the bane of this world, and that no person could endure a fourth.

My dear Sir Shrew, may Jesus shorten your life! Yet you still preach on and say than an unloved wife is reckoned to be one of these misfortunes. Are there no other kinds of comparison that you can liken your parables to, other than a poor innocent wife being one of them?

'You also compare a woman's love to hell, to barren land, where water will not dwell. You compare it also to wild fire; the more it burns, the more it has the desire to consume everything that can be burned. You say that just as worms destroy a tree, just so a wife destroys her husband; they all know this who are bound to wives.'

My lords, just in this way, as you have understood, I resolutely kept my old husbands well in hand concerning what they said in their drunkenness; and yet it was all false, but I had to call on Jankin, and also my niece as witnesses. Oh Lord! the pain and the trouble that I gave them, poor innocent things, by God's sweet suffering! For like a horse, I could bite and whinny, and I could complain, though I was in the wrong, otherwise many a time would I have been ruined. Whoever comes first to the mill, grinds first; I complained first, so our quarrel was ended.

They were ful glade to excuse hen blive
Of thing of which they nevere agilte hir live.
Of wenches wolde I beren hem on honde,
Whan that for sik unnethes mighte they stonde.
  Yet tikled I his herte, for that he
Wende that I hadde of him so greet chiertee.
I swoor that al my walkinge out by nighte
Was for t'espie wenches that he dighte;
Under that colour hadde I many a mirthe.
For al swich wit is yeven us in oure birthe;
Deceite, weping, spinning God hath yive
To wommen kindely, whil that they may live.
And thus of o thing I avaunte me,
Atte ende I hadde the bettre in ech degree,
By sleighte, or force, or by som maner thing,
As by continueel murmur or grucching.

Namely abedde hadden they meschaunce:
Ther wolde I chide, and do hem no pleasaunce;
I wolde no lenger in the bed abide,
If that I felte his arm over my side,
Til he had maad his raunson unto me;
Thanne wolde I suffre him do his nicetee.
And therfore every man this tale I telle,
Winne whoso may, for al is for to selle;
With empty hand men may none haukes lure.
For winning wolde I al his lust endure,
And make me a feyned appetit;
And yet in bacon hadde I nevere delit;
That made me that evere I wolde hem chide.

For thogh the pope hadde seten hem biside,
I wolde nat spare hem at hir owene bord;
For, by my trouthe, I quitte hem word for word.
As helpe me verray God omnipotent,
Though I right now sholde make my testament,
I ne owe hem nat a word that it nis quit.
I broghte it so aboute by my wit
That they moste yeve it up, as for the beste,
Or elles hadde we nevere been in reste.
For thogh he looked as a wood leon,
Yet sholde he faille of his conclusion.

They were jolly glad to excuse themselves forthwith for things which they had never been guilty of in their lives. I would pretend to think that they kept other women, when they were so ill they could scarcely stand.

Yet he was tickled pink as he imagined that I had such a fondness for him. I swore that all my nightly excursions were merely to search out the wenches that he consorted with; under this pretence, I had many a laugh. All such cleverness is given to us at our birth; deceit, weeping and spinning tales God has given to womankind by nature for as long as they live. And thus I can boast of one thing, in the end I got the better of them in every way, by use of cunning, or force, or in some other way, such as by continual muttering or grumbling.

Particularly they had the worst of it in bed; there I would nag them and allow them no pleasure; I would no longer stay in bed if I felt his arm creep over my side, until he had paid his ransom to me; then I would allow him to have his little treat. And, therefore, to every man I tell this tale, make what profit you can, for everything is for sale; one cannot lure a hawk back with an empty hand. In order to profit I would endure all his lust, and even pretend to have an appetite for it; and yet I never had any pleasure from old meat, and that's what made me always irritable with them.

For even though the Pope himself had sat down beside them, I would not spare them in any way, even at their own table; in truth, I paid them back word for word. So help me, True Almighty God, if I had to make my Will and Testament right now, I would not owe them a word that had not been repaid. I brought this to pass solely by my own wit and they had to give up, as the best thing to do, or otherwise we would never have been at rest. For although he might look like an enraged lion, yet he would fail in his purpose.

Thanne wolde I seye, 'Goode lief, taak keep
How mekely looketh Wilkin, oure sheep!
Com neer, my spouse, lat me ba thy cheke!
Ye sholde been al pacient and meke,
And han a sweete spiced conscience,
Sith ye so preche of Jobes pacience.
Suffreth alwey, sin ye so wel kan preche;
And but ye do, certein we shal yow teche
That it is fair to have a wyf in pees.
Oon of us two moste bowen, douteless;
And sith a man is moore resonable
Than womman is, ye moste been suffrable.

What eyleth yow to grucche thus and grone?
Is it for ye wolde have my queynte allone?
Wy, taak it al! lo, have it every deel!
Peter! I shrewe yow, but ye love it weel;
For if I wolde selle my *bele chose*,
I koude walke as fressh as is a rose;
But I wol kepe it for youre owene tooth.
Ye be to blame, by God! I sey yow sooth.'
Swiche manere wordes hadde we on honde.
Now wol I speken of my fourthe housbonde.

My fourthe housbonde was a revelour;
This is to seyn, he hadde a paramour;
And I was yong and ful of ragerie,
Stibourn and strong, and joly as a pie.
How koude I daunce to an harpe smale,
And singe, ywis, as any nightingale,
Whan I had dronke a draughte of sweete wyn!
Metellius, the foule cherl, the swyn,
That with a staf birafte his wyf hir lyf,
For she drank wyn, thogh I hadde been his wyf,
He sholde nat han daunted me fro drinke!
And after wyn on Venus moste I thinke,
For al so siker as cold engendreth hail,
A likerous mouth moste han a likerous tail.
In wommen vinolent is no defence, –
This knowen lecchours by experience.
But, Lord Crist! whan that it remembreth me
Upon my yowthe, and on my jolitee,
It tikleth me aboute myn herte roote.

Then I would say, 'My good darling, take note how meek Wilkin, our sheep, looks! Come near, my dear spouse, and let me kiss your cheek! You should be altogether patient and meek, and have a sweet clear conscience, since you preach so of Job's patience. Always be resigned, since you know how to preach so well; for unless you do, we shall certainly teach you how beautiful it is to have a wife at peace. One of us two must bow down, without any doubt; and since a man is more subject to reason than woman, you are the one who must be tolerant.

What's the matter with you that you grumble and groan so? Is it because you have my body close to yourself? Why then, take it all! Indeed, have every part of it. By Saint Peter, I could curse you, but you love it so well; for if I should happen to sell my 'belle chose', I would walk as fresh and gay as a rose; however, I will keep it safe for your own private consumption. You are to blame, by God! I tell you the truth.'

Such was the sort of bickering that we had between us. Now I will tell you about my fourth husband.

My fourth husband was a rake; that is to say, he had a mistress; and I was young and full of hot passion, stubborn and strong, and merry as a magpie. How prettily I could dance to a harp, and sing just like a nightingale when I had drunk a draught of sweet wine! Metellius, that ugly brute, that swine, who took his wife's life with a staff because she drank wine – although if I had been his wife, he would not have scared me away from drink! 'And after wine, I come to think about Venus, just as surely as cold weather brings forth hail, so a lecherous mouth must have a lecherous tail. Women, when they be full of wine, have no defence – this lechers know from experience.

But Lord Christ! When I remember about my youth, and all the merry-making, it warms the cockles of my heart.

Unto this day it dooth myn herte boote
That I have had my world as in my time.
But age, allas, that al wole envenime,
Hath me biraft my beautee and my pith.
Lat go, farewel; the devel go therwith!
The flour is goon, ther is namoore to telle;
The bren, as I best kan, now moste I selle;
But yet to be right mirie wol I fonde.
Now wol I tellen of my fourthe housbonde.
  I seye, I hadde in herte greet despit
That he of any oother had delit.
But he was quit, by God and by Seint Joce!
I made him of the same wode a croce;
Nat of my body, in no foul manere,
But certeinly, I made folk swich cheere
That in his owene grece I made him frie
For angre, and for verray jalousie.

By God! in erthe I was his purgatorie,
For which I hope his soule be in glorie.
For, God it woot, he sat ful ofte and song,
Whan that his shoo ful bitterly him wrong.
Ther was no wight, save God and he, that wiste,
In many wise, how soore I him twiste.
He deyde whan I cam fro Jerusalem,
And lith ygrave under the roode beem,
Al is his tombe noght so curius
As was the sepulcre of him Darius,
Which that Appelles wroghte subtilly;
It nis but wast to burye him preciously
Lat him fare wel, God yeve his soul reste!
He is now in his grave and in his cheste.

Now of my fifthe housbonde wol I telle.
God lete his soule nevere come in helle!
And yet was he to me the mooste shrewe;
That feele I on my ribbes al by rewe,
And evere shal unto myn ending day.
But in oure bed he was so freesh and gay,
And therwithal so wel koude he me glose,
Whan that he wolde han my *bele chose*,
That thogh he hadde me bete on every bon,
He koude winne again my love anon.

To this day it does my heart good to know that in my time I have had a world of fun. But age, alas, which poisons everything, has robbed me of my beauty and my stamina. Then let it go, farewell; and the devil go with it! The pure flour is gone, there is no more to say; the bran must I now sell as best I can; nevertheless, I shall try to be as attractive as possible. Now I will go on about my fourth husband.

I tell you, my heart was full of malice because he enjoyed himself with other women. But, by God and Saint Judocus, he was paid back in full! I carved him a cross from the same wood; mind you, not with my body in an indecent way, but by making myself so attractive to other men that I made him fry in his own grease for rage, and out of pure jealousy.

By God, I was his hell on earth, for which experience I hope his soul may now rest in heaven. For, God knows, he often sat down and cried out when the shoe pinched most painfully. There was no one, but God and himself, who knew how sorely I tormented him, and in so many ways. He died when I came back from Jerusalem, and lies buried in a grave under the cross-beam of the church. Although his tombstone is not so ornate as was the tomb of that Darius which Appelles carved so skilfully – anyway it would have been a waste to spend a lot on burying him. Fare him well, may God rest his soul! He is now safe in his grave and in his coffin.

Now I am going to tell you about my fifth husband. God will never allow his soul to be sent to hell! And yet he was to me the most unkind of them all! I can still feel the marks he made on my ribs, all along the row, and always will until my dying day. But in our bed he was so fresh and lively, and he could persuade me so easily when he wanted to have "belle chose", even though he had just beaten me on every bone, he could win my love again.

I trowe I loved him best, for that he
Was of his love daungerous to me.
We wommen han, if that I shal nat lie,
In this matere a queynte fantasie;
Waite what thing we may nat lightly have,
Thereafter wol we crie al day and crave.
Forbede us thing, and that desiren we;
Preesse on us faste, and thanne wol we fle.
With daunger oute we al oure chaffare;
Greet prees at market maketh deere ware,
And to greet cheep is holde at litel prys:
This knoweth every womman that is wys.

My fifthe housbonde, God his soule bless!
Which that I took for love, and no richesse,
He som time was a clerk of Oxenford,
And hadde left scole, and wente at hom to bord
With my gossib, dwellinge in oure toun;
God have hir soule! hir name was Alisoun.
She knew myn herte, and eek my privetee,
Bet than oure parisshe preest, so moot I thee!
To hire biwreyed I my conseil al.
For hadde myn housbonde pissed on a wal,
Or doon a thing that sholde han cost his lyf,
To hire, and to another worthy wyf,
And to my nece, which that I loved weel,
I wolde han toold his conseil every deel.
And so I dide ful often, God it woot,
That made his face often reed and hoot
For verray shame, and blamed himself for he
Had toold to me so greet a privetee.

And so bifel that ones in a Lente –
So often times I to my gossib wente,
For evere yet I loved to be gay,
And for to walke in March, Averill, and May,
Fro hous to hous, to heere sondry talis –
That Jankin clerk, and my gossib dame Alis,
And I myself, into the feeldes went.
Myn housbonde was at Londoun al that Lente;

I believe I really loved him the best, because it was not easy to make him love me. We women have, to tell the truth, a peculiar view on this subject; whatever it is that we cannot easily have, we will cry and crave after it all day long. Forbid us something, and that we will want; press something on us too strongly, however, and then away we will fly. Face us with indifference and out will come all our merchandise; a big crowd at the market makes goods more expensive, and what is too cheap is considered of little value; this is known by every woman who is wise.

My fifth husband, God bless his soul!, whom I took for love and not for his money, was at one time a student at Oxford, and after leaving University had taken board and lodging at the house of my close friend who lived in our town; God have mercy on her soul! Her name was Alison. She knew my innermost thoughts, and all my private affairs as well, even better than our parish priest, I can assure you! To her I revealed all my secrets: if my husband had pissed against a wall, or done something that could have cost his life. To her, and to another worthy woman, and to my niece, whom I loved well, I would have told every little bit of his secret, and so I did very often, God knows, and that made his face red and made him blush out of sheer shame, and he blamed himself for having told me so much of a secret.

And so it happened that during Lent – oftentimes I was wont to go and see my friend, for I always loved to be merry and gay, and to wander from house to house, in the months of March, April and May, in order to hear the local gossip – well, that student Jankin and my close friend Dame Alice, and I myself went for a walk in the fields. My husband was in London all that Lent.

I hadde the bettre leyser for to pleye,
And for to se, and eek for to be seye
Of lusty folk. What wiste I wher my grace
Was shapen for to be, or in what place?
Therfore I made my visitaciouns
To vigilies and to processiouns,
To preching eek, and to thise pilgrimages,
To pleyes of miracles, and to mariages,
And wered upon my gaye scarlet gites.
Thise wormes, ne thise motthes, ne thise mites,
Upon my peril, frete hem never a deel;
And wostow why? for they were used weel.

Now wol I tellen forth what happed me.
I seye that in the feeldes walked we,
Til trewely we hadde swich daliance,
This clerk and I, that of my purveiance
I spak to him and seyde him how that he,
If I were widwe, sholde wedde me.
For certeinly, I sey for no bobance,
Yet was I nevere withouten purveiance
Of mariage, n'of othere thinges eek.
I holde a mouses herte nat worth a leek
That hath but oon hole for to sterte to,
And if that faille, thanne is al ydo.

I bar hym on honde he hadde enchanted me, –
My dame taughte me that soutiltee.
And eek I seyde I meete of him al night,
He wolde han slain me as I lay upright,
And al my bed was ful of verray blood;
But yet I hope that he shal do me good,
For blood bitokeneth gold, as me was taught.
And al was fals; I dremed of it right naught,
But as I folwed ay my dames loore,
As wel of this as of othere thinges moore.
But now, sire, lat me se, what I shall seyn?
A ha! by God, I have my tale ageyn.

Thus I had a better opportunity to enjoy myself, to see and to be noticed by the lusty young men. How could I know where my good luck was going to come to me, or in which place? Therefore I made my visits to vigils and processions, to the sermons in the open air, and to go on these pilgrimages, and to see the miracle plays and attend the weddings, and I wore my bright scarlet gowns. These insects, neither the moths nor the mites, on my oath, never touched a bit of cloth; and do you know why? because they were used so constantly.

Now I shall go on and tell you what happened to me. I was saying that we took a walk in the fields, and truly this student and I enjoyed such love-making that I talked to him about the future, and told him that, if I were a widow, he should marry me. For certainly, and I say this as no boast, I have never been without the thought of whom I might marry in the future, or any of the other things as well. I consider that a mouse's heart is not worth a leek which has but one hole to go to and if that fails then all is lost.

I led him to believe that he had bewitched me – my mother taught me that tactic. Also I said that I had dreamed of him all through the night, and how he had wanted to kill me as I lay there stretched out, and all my bed was drenched in blood; but yet I hoped that he would be good for me, for blood signifies gold as it was taught to me. Of course, all this was quite untrue. I had dreamed nothing of the sort. I was merely following my mother's teaching, as I always did in this as in other matters.

But now Sir, let me see, what was I saying? Ah yes, by God, I have got the drift again.

Whan that my fourthe housbonde was on beere,
I weep algate, and made sory cheere,
As wives mooten, for it is usage,
And with my coverchief covered my visage,
But for that I was purveyed of a make,
I wepte but smal, and that I undertake.
To chirche was myn housbonde born a-morwe
With neighebores, that for him maden sorwe;
And Jankin, oure clerk, was oon of tho.
As help me God! whan that I saugh him go
After the beere, me thoughte he hadde a paire
Of legges and of feet so clene and faire
That al myn herte I yaf unto his hoold.
He was, I trowe, a twenty winter oold,
And I was fourty, if I shal seye sooth;
But yet I hadde alwey a coltes tooth.

Gat-tothed I was, and that bicam me weel;
I hadde the prente of seinte Venus seel.
As help me God! I was a lusty oon,
And faire, and riche, and yong, and wel bigon;
And trewely, as mine housbondes tolde me,
I hadde the beste *quoniam* mighte be.
For certes, I am al Venerien
In feelinge, and myn herte is Marcien.
Venus me yaf my lust, my likerousnesse,
And Mars yaf me my sturdy hardinesse;
Myn ascendent was Taur, and Mars therinne.

Allas, allas, that evere love was sinne!
I folwed ay myn inclinacioun
By vertu of my constellacioun;
That made me I koude noght withdrawe
My chambre of Venus from a good felawe.
Yet have I Martes mark upon my face,
And also in another privee place.
For God so wys be my salvacioun,
I ne loved nevere by no discrecioun,
But evere folwede myn appetit,
Al were he short, or long, or blak, or whit;
I took no kep, so that he liked me,
How poore he was, ne eek of what degree.

When my fourth husband was on his bier, I wept continually, and mourned deeply, as wives should, for it is the custom, and with my headscarf covering all my face; but because I already had my eyes on another mate, I did not weep too seriously, that I can assure you.

My husband was carried to church on the morrow, with all our neighbours who mourned for him; and Jankin, our clerk, was one of them. So help me God! when I saw him walk behind the coffin, I noticed that he had such a pair of legs and feet, so neat and shapely, that I completely lost my heart to him. He was, I believe, some twenty years old, and I was forty, to tell the truth; but yet I had always had a frisky nature.

Gap-toothed I was, and that became me well; I had the print and seal of Saint Venus. So help me God, I was a lusty one and fair, and rich and young and well-off; and truly, as my husbands told me, I had the best "what's it's name" that there was. For it is a fact, my feelings all come from Venus, and my heart from Mars. Venus gave me my desire and my lecherousness, and Mars gave me my sturdy stamina; I was born under Taurus, and Mars was in the sign at the time.

Alas, that ever love-making was a sin! I always followed my inclinations according to the attributes of my horoscope; which made me such that I could not withhold my little chamber of Venus from any good fellow. Yet I have the mark of Mars upon my face, and also in another private place. For as the wise God is my salvation, I never practised restraint in love-making, but always followed my appetite – be he short or tall, black or white; I did not care, as long as he liked or pleased me, how poor he was, or of what class.

What sholde I seye? but, at the monthes ende,
This joly clerk, Jankin, that was so hende,
Hath wedded me with greet solempnitee;
And to him yaf I al the lond and fee
That evere me yeven therbifoore.
But afterward repented me ful soore;
He nolde suffre nothing of my list.
By God! He smoot me ones on the list,
For that I rente out of his book a leef,
That of the strook myn ere wax al deef.
Stibourn I was as is a leonesse,
And of my tonge a verray jangleresse,
And walke I wolde, as I had doon biforn,
From hous to hous, although he had it sworn;

For which he often times wolde preche,
And me of olde Romain geestes teche;
How he Simplicius Gallus lefte his wyf,
And hire forsook for terme of al his lyf,
Noght but for open-heveded he hir say
Lookinge out at his dore upon a day.
Another Romain tolde he me by name,
That, for his wyf was at a someres game
Withouten his witing, he forsook hire eke.
And thanne wolde he upon his Bible seke
That ilke proverbe of Ecclesiaste
Where he commandeth, and forbedeth faste,
Man shal nat suffre his wyf go roule aboute
Thanne wolde he seye right thus, withouten doute:

'Whoso that buildeth his hous al of salwes,
And priketh his blinde hors over the falwes,
And suffreth his wyf to go seken halwes,
Is worthy to been hanged on the galwes!'
But al for noght, I sette noght an hawe
Of his proverbes n'of his olde sawe,
Ne I wolde nat of him corrected be.
I hate him that my vices telleth me,
And so doo mo, God woot, of us than I.
This made him with me wood al outrely;
I nolde noght forbere him in no cas.

What more can I say? Except that by the end of the month, this gay young clerk, Jankin, who was so charming, had married me with much ceremony; and I gave to him all the land and possessions that had ever been given to me previously. But afterwards I was to repent most terribly; he would not allow me to have anything I wanted. By God, he struck me once on my ear, because I had torn a leaf out of his book, and it was from that blow that my ear became all deaf. Stubborn I was, as a lioness, and as for my tongue, a proper chatterbox I was, and I went on visiting from house to house as I had done before, although he had sworn to stop it.

Because of this he would often preach at me and give me instructions from ancient Roman stories; how Simplicius Gallus left his wife, and forsook her for the rest of his life, for no other reason but that he saw her one day looking out of the door bareheaded.

He told me the name of another Roman who also, because his wife went to a summer party without his knowledge, forsook her. And then he would search through his Bible for that particular proverb in Ecclesiasticus where it commands, and strictly forbids, a man allowing his wife to go gadding about. Then invariably he would go on to say:

'Whoever builds his house all of willow branches, and spurs his blind horse over the fallow ground, and allows his wife to go visiting shrines, is fit only to be hanged on the gallows!' But it was all for nought, I cared not a fig for his proverbs, or for his old sayings, nor would I be corrected by him. I hate any man who tells me about my faults, and so, God knows, do more people than just me. This made him absolutely furious with me; as I would not give in to him in any way.

Now wol I sey yow sooth, by Seint Thomas,
Why that I rente out of his book a leef,
For which he smoot me so that I was deef.
He hadde a book that gladly, night and day,
For his desport he wolde rede alway;
He cleped it Valerie and Theofraste,
At which book he lough alwey ful faste.
And eek ther was somtime a clerk at Rome,
A cardinal, that highte Seint Jerome,
That made a book again Jovinian;
In which book eek ther was Tertulan,
Crisippus, Trotula, and Helowis,
That was abbesse nat fer fro Paris;
And eek the Parables of Salomon,
Ovides Art, and bookes many on,
And alle thise were bounden in o volume.

And every night and day was his custume,
When he hadde leyser and vacacioun
From oother worldly occupacioun,
To reden on this book of wikked wives.
He knew of hem mo legendes and lives
Than been of goode wives in the Bible.
For trusteth wel, it is an impossible
That any clerk wol speke good of wives,
But if it be of hooly seintes lives,
Ne of noon oother womman never the mo.
Who peyntede the leon, tel me who?
By God! if wommen hadde writen stories,
As clerkes han withinne hire oratories
They wolde han writen of men moore wikkednesse
Than al the mark of Adam may redresse.

The children of Mercurie and of Venus
Been in hir wirking ful contrarius;
Mercurie loveth wisdam and science,
And Venus loveth riot and dispence.
And, for hire diverse disposicioun,
Ech falleth in otheres exaltacioun.
And thus, God woot, Mercurie is desolat
In Pisces, wher Venus is exaltat;
And Venus falleth ther Mercurie is reysed.

Now I will tell you honestly, by Saint Thomas, why I tore the page out of his book, for which he struck me so that I became deaf.

He possessed a book which, night and day he would always be reading for his amusement; he called it Valerius and Theophrastus, and this book always made him laugh most heartily. And also that there was some time ago a priest at Rome, a cardinal, who was called Saint Jerome, and he wrote a treatise against Jovinian; and in this book there were references to Tertullian, Chrysippus, Trotula and Heloise, who was an abbess who once lived not far from Paris; and also the parables of Solomon, Ovid's "Art of Love" and many other books, and all these were bound in one volume.

And every night and day it was his habit, when he had some leisure and time to rest from other worldly occupations, to read about wicked women from this book. He knew more legends and life-stories of this sort than there are good women mentioned in the Bible. For believe you me, it seems an impossibility for any Churchman to speak well of women, unless it be of the living of holy saints, but never of any other kind of women. Who painted the lion, tell me who? By God, if women had written stories, like the churchmen did shut way in their little cells, then they would have written more about man's wickedness than all the race of Adam could redress.

The children of Mercury and Venus are quite contrary in disposition; the Mercury ones love wisdom and learning, while those of Venus love riot and extravagance. And because of their different disposition, each falls in its inflluence when the other is dominant. And thus, God knows, Mercury is powerless in Pisces, where Venus is dominant; and Venus loses her influence where Mercury is ascending.

Therfore no womman of no clerk is preysed.
The clerk, whan he is oold, and may noght do
Of Venus werkes worth his olde sho,
Thanne sit he doun, and writ in his dotage
That wommen kan nat kepe hir mariage.
But now to purpos, why I tolde thee
That I was beten for a book, pardee!
Upon a night Jankin, that was oure sire,
Redde on his book, as he sat by the fire,
Of Eva first, that for hir wikkednesse
Was al mankinde broght to wrecchednesse,
For which that Jhesu Crist himself was slain,
That boghte us with his herte blood again.
Lo, heere expres of womman may ye finde,
That womman was the los of al mankinde.

Tho redde he me how Sampson loste his heres:
Slepinge, his lemman kitte it with hir sheres;
Thurgh which treson loste he bothe his yen.
Tho redde he me, if that I shal nat lyen,
Of Hercules and of his Dianire,
That caused hym to sette hymself afire.
No thing forgat he the care and the wo
That Socrates hadde with has wives two;
How Xantippa caste pisse upon his heed.
This sely man sat stille as he were deed;
He wiped his heed, namoore dorste he seyn,
But "Er that thonder stinte, comth a reyn!"

Of Phasipha, that was the queene of Crete,
For shrewednesse, him thoughte the tale swete;
Fy! spek namoore – it is a grisly thyng –
Of hire horrible lust and hir liking.
Of Clitermystra, for hire lecherie,
That falsly made hire housbonde for to die,
He redde it with ful good devocioun.
He tolde me eek for what occasioun
Amphiorax at Thebes loste his lyf.
Myn housbonde hadde a legende of his wyf,
Eriphilem, that for an ouche of gold
Hath prively unto the Grekes told
Wher that hir housbonde hidde him in a place,
For which he hadde at Thebes sory grace.

This is why no scholar has praised womankind. The scholar, when he is old, and is incapable of performing the acts of Venus more than is worth an old shoe, then sits down and in his dotage writes that women cannot keep to their marriage vows.

But now to my purpose, why I told you I was beaten all because of a book, by heavens! One night, Jankin, the head of the house, read from his book as he sat by the fire; firstly about Eve, how because of her wickedness was all mankind brought to wretchedness, and on whose behalf Jesus Christ himself, who redeemed us with his own heart's blood, was slain. Look and you will find it expressly stated that woman caused the ruin of all mankind.

Then he read to me how Samson lost his hair, and how his lover cut it off with her shears whilst he was sleeping; and because of this treachery he lost both his eyes.

Then again he read to me, and I tell you no lie, about Hercules and his Deianira, who caused him to set himself on fire.

He forgot nothing of the trouble and misery that Socrates had with his two wives; how Xantippe poured piss on his head. That dear old man sat still as if he were dead; he merely wiped his head, and dared to say no more than, 'Before the thunder stops, down comes the rain!'

Next of Pasiphae, who was the queen of Crete, which, out of cussedness, he thought a delightful tale; Fie! let us speak no more – it is a grisly matter – about her horrible lust and her way of life.

Then about Clytemnestra who, because of her lechery, treacherously murdered her husband. This he read out with great seriousness.

He told me also in what circumstances Amphiaraus lost his life at Thebes. My husband had a story about his wife, Eriphyle, who for a necklace of gold secretly told the Greeks in what place her husband had hidden himself, and this is why he had such a sorry end at Thebes.

Of Livia tolde he me, and of Lucie:
They bothe made hir housbondes for to die;
That oon for love, that oother was for hate.
Livia hir housbonde, on an even late,
Empoisoned hath, for that she was his fo;
Lucia, likerous, loved hire housbonde so
That, for he sholde alwey upon hire thinke,
She yaf him swich a manere love-drinke
That he was deed er it were by the morwe;
And thus algates housbondes han sorwe.
Thanne tolde he me how oon Latumius
Compleyned unto his felawe Arrius
That in his gardin growed swich a tree
On which he seyde how that his wives thre
Hanged hemself for herte despitus.
"O leeve brother," quod this Arrius,
"Yif me a plante of thilke blissed tree,
And in my gardin planted shal it bee."

Of latter date, of wives hath he red
That somme han slain hir housbondes in hir bed,
And lete hir lecchour dighte hire al the night,
Whan that the corps lay in the floor upright.
And soome han drive nailes in hir brain,
Whil that they slepte, and thus they had hem slain.
Somme han hem yeve poisoun in hire drinke.
He spak moore harm than herte may bithinke;
And therwithal he knew of mo proverbes
Than in this world ther growen gras or herbes.
'Bet is,' quod he, 'thyn habitacioun
Be with a leon or a foul dragoun,
Than with a womman usinge for to chide.'

'Bet is,' quod he, 'hye in the roof abide,
Than with an angry wyf doun in the hous;
They been so wikked and contrarious,
They haten that hir housbondes loven ay.'
He seyde, 'a womman cast hir shame away,
Whan she cast of hir smok'; and forthermo,
'A fair womman, but she can be chaast also,
Is lyk a gold ring in a sowes nose.'
Who wolde wene, or who wolde suppose,
The wo that in myn herte was, and pine?

He told me about Livilla, and about Lucilia: how they both caused their husbands to die; the one for love, the other for hate. Livilla, late one evening, poisoned her husband because she was his enemy; the lecherous Lucilia loved her husband so much that in order that he should always be thinking about her, she gave him a love potion of such strength that he was dead before morning; and in this way husbands always seem to have a bad end.

Then he told me how one Latumius had complained to his friend Arrius that in his garden there grew a tree from which, he said, his three wives had hanged themselves from a broken heart. 'My dear brother', said this Arrius, 'give me a cutting of that blessed tree, and it shall be planted in my garden.'

From later times, he read out about some wives some of whom had slain their husbands in their beds, and let their lovers lie with them all night while the corpse lay stretched out on the floor. And some had driven nails in their brains while they were sleeping, and in this way they slew them. And some had given their husbands poison in their drink. He spoke more malice than the heart could imagine; and, in addition, he knew of more proverbs than there are blades of grass or herbs in all this world. 'It is better,' he said, 'if one were to live together with a lion or even a foul dragon, than with a woman whose habit it is to scold.'

'It is better,' he went on, 'to live high up in the roof, than with an angry wife down below in the house; they are so wicked and contrary that they will always hate what their husbands love.' He continued, 'A woman casts her shame away every time she takes off her smock,' and furthermore, 'a beautiful woman, unless she is also chaste, is like a gold ring in a pig's snout'. Who could think, or who could imagine, the misery and the agony that was in my heart?

And whan I saugh he wolde nevere fine
To reden on this cursed book al night,
Al sodeynly thre leves have I plight
Out of his book, right as he radde, and eke
I with my fest so took him on the cheke
That in oure fyr he fil bakward adoun.
And he up stirte as dooth a wood leoun,
And with his fest he smoot me on the heed,
That in the floor I lay as I were deed.
And whan he saugh how stille that I lay,
He was agast, and wolde han fled his way,
Til atte laste out of my swogh I breyde.
'O, hastow slain me, false theef?' I seyde,
'And for my land thus hastow mordred me?
Er I be deed, yet wol I kisse thee.'

And neer he cam, and kneled faire adoun,
And seyde, 'Deere suster Alisoun,
As help me God! I shal thee nevere smite.
That I have doon, it is thyself to wite.
Foryeve it me, and that I thee biseke!'
And yet eftsoones I hitte him on the cheke,
And seyde, 'Theef, thus muchel am I wreke;
Now wol I die, I may no lenger speke.'
But atte laste, with muchel care and wo,
We fille acorded by us selven two.
He yaf me al the bridel in myn hond,
To han the governance of hous and lond,
And of his tonge, and of his hond also;
And made him brenne his book anon right tho.

And whan that I hadde geten unto me,
By maistrie, al the soverainetee,
And that he seyde, 'Myn owene trewe wyf,
Do as thee lust the terme of al thy lfy;
Keep thyn honour, and keep eek myn estäat' –
After that day we hadden never debaat.
God helpe me so, I was to him as kinde
As any wyf from Denmark unto Inde,
And also trewe, and so was he to me.
I prey to God, that sit in magestee,
So blesse his soule for his mercy deere.
Now wol I seye my tale, if ye wol heere.

And when I realized that he would never stop reading from this cursed book all night, I suddenly pulled three pages out of the book, as he was reading it, and also with my fist I struck him on the cheek so that he fell down backwards into the fireplace. He jumped up like a mad lion and with his fist he struck me on the head so that I collapsed on the floor as if I were dead. And when he realized how still I lay, he was horrified, and would have run away, if I had not at last started from my swoon. 'Oh, have you slain me, false thief?' I shouted, 'and was it for my land that you have murdered me? And yet, before I die, I do want to kiss you.'

He came close, and knelt down softly beside me, and said, 'Dear Sister Alison, so help me God, I shall never strike you again! What I have done, it is you who are to blame. Forgive me for it, this I do beseech you!' And with that I suddenly hit him on the cheek, and cried, 'Thief, this much am I revenged; now I will die, I can no longer speak.' But at last, with much care and woe, we came to an agreement between our two selves. He gave the bridle back into my hand, to have all the control over the house and the land, and of his tongue and of his hand as well; and I made him burn his book right there.

And when, by my superior wit, I had got all the sovereignty for myself, and he had promised, 'my own true wife, you do as you want for the rest of your life; but keep hold of your honour, and take care of my reputation' – after that day we never had another argument. So help me God, I was as kind to him as any wife from Denmark to India, and as true, as he was to me. I pray to God, who sits in majesty, so to bless his soul for His dear mercy's sake. Now I shall tell my tale, if you still want to hear it.

The Frere lough, whan he hadde herd al this;
'Now dame,' quod he, 'so have I joye or blis,
This is a long preamble of a tale!'
And whan the Somonour herde the Frere gale,
'Lo,' quod the Somonour, 'Goddes armes two!
A frere wol entremette him everemo.
Lo, goode men, a flie and eek a frere
Wol falle in every dissh and eek mateere.
What spekestow of preambulacioun?
What! amble, or trotte, or pees, or go sit doun!
Thou lettest oure disport in this manere.'
'Ye, woltow so, sire Somonour?' quod the Frere;
'Now, by my feith, I shal, er that I go,
Telle of a somonour swich a tale or two,
That alle the folk shall laughen in this place.'

'Now elles, Frere, I bishrewe thy face,'
Quod this Somonour, 'and I bishrewe me,
But if I telle tales two or thre
Of freres, er I come to Sidingborne,
That I shal make thyn herte for to morne,
For wel I woot thy pacience is gon.'
Oure Hooste cride 'Pees! and that anon!'
And seyde, 'Lat the womman telle hire tale.
Ye fare as folk that dronken ben of ale.
Do, dame, telle forth youre tale, and that is best.'
'Al redy, sire,' quod she, 'right as yow lest,
If I have licence of this worthy Frere.'
'Yis, dame,' quod he, 'tel forth, and I wol heere.'

The Friar laughed aloud, when he had heard all this; 'Now Madam,' he said, 'as I may have joy or bliss, this is a long preamble to a tale!' And when the Summoner heard the Friar say this, he shouted, 'Lo, by God's two arms, a friar will always be interrupting. Lo good people, both a fly and a friar will fall upon every dish and every business. What do you mean when you speak of "perambulation"? Why don't you just amble around, or take a walk, or shut up and go and sit down! You are interfering with our pleasure with your interruption.'

'Oh, say you so, Sir Summoner?' growled the Friar, 'now by my faith, before I'm finished, I shall tell such a tale or two about a Summoner that will make all the people in this place roar with laughter'.

'As for that, Friar, I curse your mouth', the Summoner answered back, 'and I shall curse myself if I do not tell two or three tales about you friars, before I come to Sittingbourne, which will make you writhe in your heart, for I know only too well that you have lost your temper.'

Our Host cried out, 'Be quiet! and at once!' then he went on, 'let the woman tell her tale. You two are behaving like someone drunk with ale Go on, Madam, proceed to tell your tale, that will be the best way.'

'All ready, Sir,' she said, 'just as you please, that is if I have the permission of this worthy Friar.'

'Indeed you do, Madam,' he replied, 'tell forth, and I will listen.'

The Wife of Bath's Tale

In th'olde dayes of the King Arthour,
Of which that Britons speken greet honour,
Al was this land fulfild of faierie.
The elf-queene, with hir joly compaignie,
Daunced ful ofte in many a grene mede.
This was the olde opinion, as I rede;
I speke of manie hundred yeres ago.
But now kan no man se none elves mo,
For now the grete charitee and prayeres
Of limitours and othere hooly freres,
That serchen every lond and every streem,
As thikke as motes in the sonne-beem,
Blessinge halles, chambres, kichenes, boures,
Citees, burghes, castels, hye toures,
Thropes, bernes, shipnes, daieries –
This maketh that ther ben no faieries.

For ther as wont to walken was an elf,
Ther walketh now the limitour himself,
In undermeles and in morweninges,
And seyth his matins and his hooly thinges
As he gooth in his limitacioun.
Wommen may go now saufly up and doun.
In every bussh or under every tree
Ther is noon oother incubus but he,
And he ne wol doon hem but dishonour.

And so bifel it that this king Arthour
Hadde in his hous a lusty bacheler,
That on a day cam ridinge fro river;
And happed that, allone as he was born,
He saugh a maide walkinge him biforn,
Of which maide anon, maugree hir heed,
By verray force, he rafte hire maidenhed;

The Wife of Bath's Tale

In the olden days of King Arthur, of whom the Britons speak with great reverence, this land was all filled with fairies. The fairy queen, with her merry company, danced often in many a green meadow. Anyway, this was the old popular belief, as I understand it – I speak of many hundred years ago. But now no one can see the fairies anymore, for the great beneficence and the prayers of mendicants and other holy friars who search out every field and every stream, as thick as spots of dust in the sunbeam, blessing halls, chambers, kitchens, bedrooms, cities, boroughs, castles and high towers, villages, barns, stables and dairies – and because of this there are now no fairies around.

For where an elf used to walk, now walks the limiter himself, in the afternoons and in the mornings, saying his matins and his holy business, as he goes about within his district. And now women may walk abroad quite safely as in every bush or under every tree, there is no other incubus but he, and he will do nothing more than deflower them.

And so it happened that this King Arthur had in his household a lusty young knight, who one day came riding up from the river; and it happened that while he was riding all alone, he saw a maiden walking ahead of him, and from that maiden, against her will and by brute force, he promptly took her maidenhead.

For which oppressioun was swich clamour
And swich pursute unto the king Arthour,
That dampned was this knight for to be deed,
By cours of lawe, and sholde han lost his heed –
Paraventure swich was the statut tho –
But that the queene and othere ladies mo
So longe preyeden the king of grace,
Til he his lyf him graunted in the place,
And yaf him to the queene, al at hir wille,
To chese wheither she wolde him save or spille.
The queene thanketh the king with al hir might,
And after this thus spak she to the knight,
Whan that she saugh hir time, upon a day:
'Thou standest yet,' quod she, 'in swich array
That of thy lyf yet hastow no suretee.

I grante thee lyf, if hou kanst tellen me
What thing is it that wommen moost desiren.
Be war, and keep thy nekke-boom from iren!
And if thou kanst nat tellen it anon,
Yet wol I yeve thee leve for to gon
A twelf-month and a day, to seche and leere
An answere suffisant in this mateere;
And suretee wol I han, er that thou pace,
Thy body for to yelden in this place.'
Wo was this knight, and sorwefully he siketh;
But what, he may nat do al as him liketh.
And at the laste he chees him for to wende,
And come again, right at the yeres ende,
With swich answere as God wolde him purveye;
And taketh his leve, and wendeth forth his weye.

He seketh every hous and every place
Where as he hopeth for to finde grace,
To lerne what thing wommen loven moost;
But he ne koude arriven in no coost
Wher as he mighte finde in this mateere
Two creatures accordinge in-feere.
Somme seyde wommen loven best richesse,
Somme seyde honour, somme seyde jolinesse,
Somme riche array, soome seyden lust abedde,
And oftetime to be widwe and wedde.

This act of violence caused such a clamour and such petition to King Arthur that this knight was condemned to death, according to the law, and should have lost his head – as it happened such was the statute at that time – but the Queen and some other ladies so pressingly begged the King for mercy that he granted him his life there and then, and gave him over to the Queen, to do anything that she wanted with him, to choose whether she would save or seal his doom.

The Queen thanked the King with all her power, and after she spoke thus to the knight, one day when she saw that the time was right: 'You still stand,' she said, 'in such a situation that you have no certainty about keeping your life.

I will grant you your life, if you can tell me what thing it is that women most desire. Be very careful, and keep your neck away from the iron blade! And if you cannot give the answer immediately, then I will give you leave to go away for a year and a day, to seek and find out a satisfactory answer in this matter; and a promise I will have, before you go away, that you will give up your person again in this place.'

Sad was the knight, and sorrowfully he sighed; but then he had no choice to do otherwise. And in the end, he chose to go off, and come back again right at the end of the year, with such an answer as God would provide him with; and he took his leave, and went forth on his way.

He searched out every house and every place where he hoped to find some chance to learn what thing women love most; but he could come to no coast where he could find on this subject two people who agreed together. Some said women loved riches best, some said honour, some said entertainment, some rich attire, some said the pleasures of the bed, and others to be widowed often and re-married.

Somme seyde that oure hertes been moost esed
Whan that we been yflatered and yplesed.
He gooth ful ny the sothe, I wol nat lie.
A man shal winne us best with flaterie;
And with attendance, and with bisinesse,
Been we ylimed, bothe moore and lesse.
And somme seyen that we loven best
For to be free, and do right as us lest,
And that no man repreve us of oure vice,
But seye that we be wise, and no thing nice.
For trewely ther is noon of us alle,
If any wight wol clawe us on the galle,
That we nel kike, for he seith us sooth.
Assay, and he shal finde it that so dooth;
For, be we never so vicious withinne,
We wol been holden wise and clene of sinne.

And somme seyn that greet delit han we
For to been holden stable, and eek secree,
And in o purpos stedefastly to dwelle,
And nat biwreye thing that men us telle.
But that tale is nat worth a rake-stele.
Pardee, we wommen konne no thing hele;
Witnesse on Mida, – wol ye heere the tale?
Ovide, amonges othere thinges smale,
Seyde Mida hadde, under his longe heres,
Growing upon his heed two asses eres,
The whiche vice he hidde, as he best mighte,
Ful subtilly from every mannes sighte,
That, save his wyf, ther wiste of it namo.
He loved hire moost, and trusted hire also;
He preyede hire that to no creature
She sholde tellen of his disfigure.

She swoor him nay, for al this world to winne,
She nolde do that vileynie or sinne,
To make hir housbonde han so foul a name.
She nolde nat telle it for hir owene shame.
But nathelees, hir thoughte that she dide,
That she so longe sholde a conseil hide;
Hir thoughte it swal so soore aboute hir herte
That nedely som word hire moste asterte;

Some said that our hearts are most comforted when we are flattered and gratified. This comes very near the truth, I will not lie. A man will best win us with flattery; and with attention and with homage are we possessed, both the high and the low.

And some said that we love best to be free and to do just as we please, and that no man should reproach us for our weaknesses, but declare that we are wise and in no way foolish. For truly, there is not one of us, if anyone should scratch us in a sore place by telling us the truth about ourselves, who will not kick back. Let him try it, and he shall find that this is so; for no matter how bad we are inside, we want to be thought of as wise and devoid of sin.

And some say that we take great delight in being considered reliable, and discreet as well, and to stick steadfastly to our resolve, and not betray anything that people tell us in confidence. But that opinion is not worth an old handle. My goodness, we women can really keep nothing concealed; witness Midas – would you like to hear the story?

Ovid, amongst other small matters, told that Midas had, under his long hair, two ass's ears growing out of his head, which deformity he concealed, as best he could, most carefully from everyone's sight, so that no one knew of it, except his wife. He loved her most dearly, and trusted her as well; he begged her not to tell anybody of his disfigurement.

She swore to him that she would not, even if it were to gain the whole world, commit any disloyalty or wickedness to make her husband get so bad a name. In fact, she could not reveal it because of her own shame. But nevertheless, she thought that she would die if she had to keep the secret for very long; it seemed to her that it swelled so hard about her heart that from necessity some information must leak out.

And sith she dorste telle it to no man,
Doun to a mareys faste by she ran –
Til she cam there, hir herte was a-fire –
And as a bitore bombleth in the mire,
She leyde hir mouth unto the water doun:
'Biwreye me nat, thou water, with thy soun,'
Quod she; 'to thee I telle it and namo;
Myn housbonde hath longe asses eris two!
Now is myn herte at hool, now is it oute.
I myghte no lenger kepe it, out of doute.'
Heere may ye se, thogh we a time abide,
Yet out it moot; we kan no conseil hide.
The remenant of the tale if ye wol heere,
Redeth Ovide, and ther ye may it leere.

This knight, of which my tale is specially,
Whan that he saugh he mighte nat come therby –
This is to seye, what wommen love moost –
Withinne his brest ful sorweful was the goost.
But hoom he gooth, he mighte nat sojourne;
The day was come that homward moste he tourne.
And in his wey it happed him to ride,
In al this care, under a forest side,
Wher as he saugh upon a daunce go
Of ladies foure and twenty, and yet mo;
Toward the whiche daunce he drow ful yerne,
In hope that som wisdom sholde he lerne.
But certeinly, er he cam fully there,
Vanisshed was this daunce, he niste where.

No creature saugh he that bar lyf,
Save on the grene he saugh sittinge a wyf;
A fouler wight ther may no man devise.
Again the knight this olde wyf gan rise,
And seyde, 'Sire knight, heer forth ne lith no wey.
Tel me what that ye seken, by youre fey!'
Paraventure it may the bettre be;
Thise olde folk kan muchel thing,' quod she.
'My leeve mooder,' quod this knight, 'certeyn
I nam but deed, but if that I kan seyn
What thing it is that wommen moost desire.
Koude ye me wisse, I wolde wel quite youre hire.'

And since she dare not tell it to anybody, she ran down to the marsh close by – her heart was on fire until she got there – and as a bittern booms in the mudflat, she put her mouth down into the water: 'Betray me not, you water, with your sound,' she said, 'to you I will tell my secret and to no one else; my husband has two long ass's ears! Now is my heart relieved, now the secret is out. I could not keep it in any longer, without a doubt.' Here you can see, although we might wait for some time, yet it must come out; we just cannot hide a secret. If you wish to hear the rest of the story, then read Ovid, and there you can learn it all.

When this knight, whom my tale particularly concerns, saw that he could not come by it, – that is to say, what women love most – the spirit in his breast was very dejected. Nevertheless, home he went, for he could not linger any longer; for the day had come when homewards must he turn. And on his way, with all his worry, he chanced to ride along the side of a forest where he saw moving in a dance four and twenty ladies, or even more; and towards the dance he approached most eagerly in the hope that he might learn something of the wisdom that he was seeking. But, indeed, before he quite got there the dancers vanished, he knew not where.

No one did he see who was a living creature, except he did see sitting on the greensward one old woman; a more ugly person no one could imagine. The old woman got up to meet the knight and said, 'Sir Knight, no way goes on from here. Tell me, by your faith, what are you looking for? Perhaps it may be for the better; we old ones know quite a lot of things' she said.

'My dear mother,' the Knight replied, 'I am certainly as good as dead unless I am able to tell what thing it is that women most desire. If you could give me some indication of it, I would well repay the favour.'

'Plight me thy trouthe heere in my hand,' quod she,
'The nexte thing that I requere thee,
Thou shalt it do, if it lie in thy might,
And I wol telle it yow er it be night.'
'Have heer my trouthe,' quod the knight, 'I grante.'
'Thanne,' quod she, 'I dar me wel avante
Thy lyf is sauf; for I wol stonde therby,
Upon my lyf, the queene wol seye as I.
Lat se which is the proudeste of hem alle,
That wereth on a coverchief or a calle,
That dar seye nay of that I shal thee teche.
Lat us go forth, withouten lenger speche.'
Tho rowned she a pistel in his ere,
And bad him to be glad, and have no fere.

When they be comen to the court, this knight
Seyde he had holde his day, as he hadde hight,
And redy was his answere, as he sayde.
Ful many a noble wyf, and many a maide,
And many a widwe, for that they been wise,
The queene hirself sittinge as a justise,
Assembled been, his answere for to heere;
And afterward this knight was bode appeere.
To every wight commanded was silence,
And that the knight sholde telle in audience
What thing that worldly wommen loven best.
This knight ne stood nat stille as doth a best,
But to his questioun anon answerde
With manly vois, that al the court it herde:

'My lige lady, generally,' quod he,
'Wommen desiren to have sovereinetee
As wel over hir housbond as hir love,
And for to been in maistrie him above.
This is youre nooste desir, thogh ye me kille.
Dooth as yow list; I am heer at youre wille.'
In al the court ne was ther wyf, ne maide,
Ne widwe, that contraried that he saide,
But seyden he was worthy han his lyf.
And with that word up stirte the olde wyf,
Which that the knight saugh sittinge on the grene:
'Mercy,' quod she, 'my soverein lady queene!
Er that youre court departe, do me right.

'Pledge me your word, here upon my hand,' she said, 'that the next thing that I require of you, you will do it, if it lies in your power, and then I will tell you the answer before it is night.'

'You have here my word' the Knight replied, 'I grant it to you.'

'Then,' she said, 'I dare to boast openly that your life is quite safe; for I will stand by it, on my life, that the queen will say as I do. Let us see whether the proudest of all those who wear a headscarf or head-dress would dare to deny what I am going to teach you. Now let's go on our way without any more talk.' With this she whispered some information in his ear, and bade him to be happy and to have no fear.

When they had come to the court, the Knight announced that he had kept to his date as he had promised, and that he had his answer ready, as best he could. Many a noble wife, many a maid, and many a widow (for they are considered very wise), with the queen herself sitting as judge, were assembled to hear his answer; and soon afterwards the Knight was summoned to appear.

Every person was commanded to be silent, and the Knight was told to tell in their hearing what thing it was that women in the world loved best. This Knight did not stand fixed like a beast, but answered the question directly in a confident and clear voice so that all the court heard it:

'My liege lady,' he said, 'in general terms, women desire to have sovereignty over their husbands as well as their lovers, and to have mastery over them. This is your greatest desire, though you may kill me for it. Do as you please; I am here at your will!' In all the court there was neither wife, maiden nor widow who contradicted what he said, but all said that he deserved to have his life. And at that word up jumped the old woman, the one the Knight had seen sitting on the greensward: 'Mercy', she cried, 'my sovereign lady queen! Before your court disperses, give me my due.

I taughte this answere unto the knight;
For which he plighte me his trouthe there,
The firste thing that I wolde him requere,
He wolde it do, if it lay in his mighte.
Bifore the court thanne preye I thee, sir knight,'
Quod she, 'that thou me take unto thy wyf;
For wel thou woost that I have kept thy lyf.
If I seye fals, sey nay, upon thy fey!'
   This knight answerde, 'Allas, and weilawey!
I woot right wel that swich was my biheste.
For Goddes love, as chees a newe requeste;
Taak al my good, and lat my body go.'

   'Nay, thanne,' quod she, 'I shrewe us bothe two!
For thogh that I be foul, and oold, and poore,
I nolde for al the metal, ne for oore,
That under erthe is grave, or lith above,
But if thy wyf I were, and eek thy love.'
   'My love?' quod he, 'nay, my dampnacioun!
Allas, that any of my nacioun
Sholde evere so foule disparaged be!'
But al for nought; the ende is this, that he
Constreined was, he nedes moste hire wedde;
And taketh his olde wyf, and gooth to bedde.

   Now wolden som men seye, paraventure,
That for my necligence I do no cure
To tellen yow the joye and al th'array
That at the feeste was that ilke day.
To which thing shortly answeren I shal:
I seye ther nas no joye ne feeste at al;
Ther nas but heviness and much sorwe.
For prively he wedded hire on the morwe,
And al day after hidde him as an owle,
So wo was him, his wyf looked so foule.
   Greet was the wo the knight hadde in his thoght,
Whan he was with his wyf abedde ybroght;
He walweth and he turneth to and fro,
His olde wyf lay smilinge everemo,
And seyde, 'O deere housbonde, *benedicitee!*
Fareth every knight thus with his wyf as ye?
Is this the lawe of King Arthures hous?
Is every knight of his so dangerous?

I taught the answer to the knight: and for that he pledged his solemn word at the time that the first thing that I would require of him, he would do if it lay in his power. Before this court I ask you then, Sir Knight,' she went on, 'to take me for your wife; for well you know that I have saved your life. If I say false, deny it, on your faith!'

The Knight answered, 'Alas, and woe is me! I know very well that such was my promise. But for the love of God, choose another request; take all my goods, but let my body go!'

'Oh no', she cried, 'a curse on both of us! For although I am ugly, and old and poor, I would not want all the metal or the ore that is buried under the earth, or that lies above it, unless I were thy wife, and thy very love as well.'

'My very love?' he cried, 'Indeed no, it would be my damnation! Alas, that anyone of my family background should ever be as dreadfully disgraced!' But it was all for nothing; in the end he was forced to agree that he was obliged to wed her; and he took his old wife and went to bed.

Now some people might say, perhaps, that out of neglect I do not take the trouble to describe to you the joy and all the celebration that took place at the feasting on that day. If so, I shall answer in short: I say that there was no rejoicing or feasting at all: there was nothing but heaviness of heart and much sorrow. He secretly married her the next day, and all day afterwards he hid himself away like an owl, so unhappy was he because his wife looked so ugly.

Great was the distress that the Knight had in his thoughts when he was brought with his wife to bed; he tossed and he turned to and fro. His old wife lay smiling all this time, and then said, 'Oh dear husband, bless my soul! Does every knight behave in this way with his wife as you do? Is this the conduct for those of King Arthur's household? Is every Knight of his so indifferent?

I am youre owene love and eek youre wyf:
I am she which that saved hath youre lyf,
And, certes, yet ne dide I yow nevere unright;
Why fare ye thus with me this firste night?
Ye faren lyk a man had lost his wit.
What is my gilt? For Goddes love, tel me it,
And it shal been amended, if I may.'
'Amended?' quod this knight, 'allas, nay, nay!
It wol hat been amended nevere mo.
Thou art so loothly, and so oold also,
And therto comen of so lough a kinde,
That litel wonder is thogh I walwe and winde.
So wolde God myn herte wolde breste!'

'Is this,' quod she, 'the cause of youre unreste?'
'Ye, certeinly,' quod he, 'no wonder is.'
'Now, sire,' quod she, 'I koude amende al this,
If that me liste, er it were dayes thre,
So wel ye mighte bere yow unto me.
'But, for ye speken of swich gentillesse
As is descended out of old richesse,
That therfore sholden ye be gentil men,
Swich arrogance is nat worth an hen.
Looke who that is moost vertuous alway,
Privee and apert, and moost entendeth ay
To do the gentil dedes that he kan;
Taak him for the grettest gentil man.

Crist wole we claime of him oure gentillesse,
Nat of oure eldres for hire old richesse.
For thogh they yeve us al hir heritage,
For which we claime to been of heigh parage
Yet may they nat biquethe, for no thing,
To noon of us hir vertuous living,
That made hem gentil men ycalled be,
And bad us folwen hem in swich degree.
'Wel kan the wise poete of Florence,
That highte Dant, speken in this sentence.
Lo, in swich maner rym is Dantes tale:
"Ful selde up riseth by his branches smale
Prowesse of man, for God, of his goodnesse,
Wole that of him we claime oure gentillesse";
For of oure eldres may we no thing claime
But temporel thing, that man may hurte and maime.

I am your own beloved and your wife; and I am the one who saved your life, and certainly, I never did you any wrong. Why then do you behave to me in this way on our first night together? You act like a person who has gone out of his mind. What am I guilty of? For God's love, tell me and I shall put it right, if I possibly can'.

'Put it right?' the Knight replied, 'Alas, no never! It will never be put right ever again. You are so loathsome and so old as well, and moreover you come from such low kin that it is little wonder that I toss and turn about. Would to God my heart would burst!'

'Is this,' she said, 'the cause of your unrest?'

'Yes certainly,' he replied, 'and no wonder either'.

'Now Sir,' she said, 'I could put all this right if I wanted to, before three days have passed, if you were only to behave nicely to me.

'But you spoke of the good manners and breeding which is inherited from ancient rank and estate, and because of this you feel that you should be considered a gentleman – such arrogance is not worth a hen! Look around you and see who is always the most virtuous, both in private and in public, and who always intends to behave like a gentleman, wherever he can; he is the one to take as the greatest gentleman.

Christ wants us to claim our gentility from Him, not from our ancestors because of their ancient inheritance, from which we claim our high descent; yet they cannot in any way bequeath to any of us their virtuous way of life, which made them rightly to be called gentlemen, and in which standard they instructed us to follow them.

'Well can that wise poet of Florence, the one called Dante, speak on this subject. Dante's comments are contained in the following lines: "Seldom by the small branches of the family tree does man's nobility rise up, for God in his goodness, wills that we claim our gentility from Him"; for from our ancestors we can claim nothing but temporal things, and with these man may hurt and maim.

'Eek every wight woot this as wel as I,
If gentillesse were planted natureelly
Unto a certeyn linage doun the line,
Privee and apert, thanne wolde they nevere fine
To doon of gentilesse the faire office;
They mighte do no vileynie or vice.
'Taak fyr, and ber it in the derkeste hous
Bitwix this and the mount of Kaukasous,
And lat men shette the dores and go thenne;
Yet wole the fyr as faire lie and brenne
As twenty thousand men mighte it biholde;
His office natureel ay wol it holde,
Up peril of my lyf, til that it die

'Heere may ye se wel how that genterie
Is nat annexed to possessioun,
Sith folk ne doon hir operacioun
Alwey, as dooth the fyr, lo, in his kinde.
For, God it woot, men may wel often finde
A lordes sone do shame and vileynie;
And he that wole han pris of his gentrie,
For he was boren of a gentil hous,
And hadde his eldres noble and vertuous,
And nel himselven do no gentil dedis,
Ne folwen his gentil auncestre that deed is,
He nis nat gentil, be he duc or erl;
For vileyns sinful dedes make a cherl.

Thy gentillesse nis but renomee
Of thine auncestres, for hire heigh bountee,
Which is a strange thing to thy persone.
For gentillesse cometh fro God allone.
Thanne comth oure verray gentillesse of grace;
It was no thing biquethe us with oure place.
'Thenketh hou noble, as seith Valerius,
Was thilke Tullius Hostillius,
That out of poverte roos to heigh noblesse.
Reedeth Senek, and redeth eek Boece;
Ther shul ye seen expres that it no drede is
That he is gentil that dooth gentil dedis.

'Also, everyone knows as well as I do that if good manners and breeding were implanted by nature in direct lineage down the line of descent, then those people would never hesitate, in private or in public, to do the fair duty of a gentleman; if so, they could never do anything villainous or offensive.

'Take fire, and carry it to the darkest house between this place and the Mount of Caucasus, and let men shut the doors and go away, yet the fire will blaze and burn as brightly as if twenty thousand men were watching it; its natural function will it always obey, I bet my life on it, until it dies.

'From this you can well see how noble conduct is not a consequence of estate, since people do not carry out their natural functions always, as the fire does according to its nature. For, God knows, one may very often find a lord's son doing shameful and villainous things; and he who wants to have the advantages of a good family background, having been born of a noble house and because his forbears were noble and virtuous, and yet he himself is not prepared to behave like a gentleman, or follow the conduct of his noble ancestor who is now dead, then he is no gentleman, be he duke or earl; for villainous and shameful deeds make him a churl.

Your gentility is nothing but the reputation of your ancestors, being derived from their illustrious repute, all of which is foreign to your person. For real gentility comes from God alone. From Him comes the true nobility of grace; and in no way is it handed down to us according to our position.

'Just think how noble, as Valerius tells us, was that Tullius Hostilius, who rose out of poverty to high nobility. Read Seneca, and comprehend Boethius too; there you will see it made clear, without any doubt, that he is only a gentleman who acts like a gentleman.

And therfore, leeve housbonde, I thus conclude:
Al were it that mine auncestres were rude,
Yet may the hye God, and so hope I,
Grante me grace to liven vertuously.
Thanne am I gentil, whan that I biginne
To liven vertuously and weive sinne.
  'And ther as ye of poverte me repreeve,
The hye God, on whom that we bileeve,
In wilful poverte chees to live his lyf.
And certes every man, maiden, or wyf,
May understonde that Jhesus, hevene king,
Ne wolde nat chese a vicious living.
Glad poverte is an honest thing, certeyn;
This wole Senec and othere clerkes seyn.

Whoso that halt him paid of his poverte,
I holde him riche, al hadde he nat a sherte.
He that coveiteth is a povre wight,
For he wolde han that is nat in his might;
But he that noght hath, ne coveiteth have,
Is riche, although ye holde him but a knave.
Verray poverte, it singeth proprely;
Juvenal seith of poverte mirily:
"The povre man, whan he goth by the weye,
Bifore the theves he may singe and pleye."
Poverte is hateful good and, as I gesse,
A ful greet bringere-out of bisinesse;
A greet amendere eek of sapience
To him that taketh it in pacience.

Poverte is this, although it seme alenge,
Possessioun that no wight wol chalenge.
Poverte ful ofte, whan a man is lowe,
Maketh his God and eek himself to knowe.
Poverte a spectacle is, as thinketh me,
Thurgh which he may his verray freendes see.
And therfore, sire, sin that I noght yow greve,
Of my poverte namoore ye me repreve.

And, therefore, dear husband, I thus conclude; although my ancestors were indeed low-born, yet may the God on high, and it is my sincere hope, grant me that grace to live virtuously. Then I will be a gentlewoman, when I start to live virtuously and refrain from sin.

'And as for the poverty you reproach me for, the high God in whom we all believe, in poverty purposely chose to live his life. And certainly every man, maiden or wife can understand that Jesus, Heaven's King, would not choose a shameful way of living. To be poor and happy is an honest way to live, for sure; all this is said by Seneca and other learned men.

Whoever considers himself satisfied in his poverty, I hold him to be rich, even though he had no shirt on his back. He who covets possessions is indeed a poor man, for he would have that which is not in his power to have; but he who has nothing, nor wants anything, is indeed rich, although you would hold him but a serf. True poverty sings its own tune; Juvenal says some good things about poverty: "The poor man, when he goes on his way, can sing and relax in the presence of thieves." Poverty is both good and bad, and I have a good idea that it is the greatest bringer-out of diligence; a great improver of wisdom to him who accepts it patiently.

Poverty is all this, though it may seem miserable, it is certainly an acquisition that no man will challenge you for. Poverty will very often, when a man is dejected, make him know both his God and himself better. Poverty can, it seems to me, be considered as a pair of spectacles, through which a man may identify his true friends. And, therefore, sir, since that because of it I do you no harm, do not then you reproach me any more about my poverty.

Now, sire, of elde ye repreve me;
And certes, sire, thogh noon auctoritee
Were in no book, ye gentils of honour
Seyn that men sholde an oold wight doon favour,
And clepe him fader, for youre gentillesse;
And auctours shal I finden, as I gesse.

'Now ther ye seye that I am foul and old,
Than drede you noght to been a cokewold;
For filthe and eelde, also moot I thee,
Been grete wardeyns upon chastitee.
But nathelees, sin I knowe youre delit,
I shal fulfille youre worldly appetit.
'Chese now,' quod she, 'oon of thise thinges tweye:
To han me foul and old til that I deye,
And be to yow a trewe, humble wyf,
And nevere yow displese in al my lyf;
Or elles ye wol han me yong and fair,
And take youre aventure of the repair
That shal be to youre hous by cause of me,
Or in som oother place, may wel be.
Now chese yourselven, wheither that yow liketh.'

This knight aviseth him and sore siketh,
But atte laste he seyde in this manere:
'My lady and my love, and wyf so deere,
I put me in youre wise governance;
Cheseth yourself which may be moost plesance,
And moost honour to yow and me also.
I do no fors the wheither of the two;
For as yow liketh, it suffiseth me.'
'Thanne have I gete of yow maistrie,' quod she,
'Sin I may chese and governe as me lest?'
'Ye, certes, wyf,' quod he, 'I holde it best.'
'Kis me,' quod she, 'we be no lenger wrothe;
For, by my trouthe, I wol be to yow bothe,
This is to seyn, ye, bothe fair and good.

'Now, sir, you also reproach me for my old age; and certainly sir, if there was no authoritative statement on the matter in any book, you gentlemen of honour state that men should behave courteously towards an old person, and call him father, because of your good breeding; and authors I can find to subscribe to this, I think.'

'Now you also state that I am ugly and old, in which case you should have no dread about being a cuckold; for foulness and old age, as I believe, are great guardians of chastity. But nevertheless, since I know what you desire, I shall satisfy your worldly appetites.

'Choose now,' she said, 'one of these two things: either to have me ugly and old until I die, and be yet a faithful and humble wife to you, and never displease you in all my life; or else to have me young and fair, and take your chance about what resort your house is put to because of me, or in some other place, it could well be. Now choose for yourself, whichever you like.'

The Knight thought hard, and sighed deeply, but at last he spoke out in the following way: 'My lady and my love, and my wife so dear, I shall put myself under your wise government; you choose yourself which is the most pleasant way, and the most honourable for you and me as well. It does not matter to me which of the two it is; for whatever pleases you, will satisfy me.'

'Then have I got the mastery over you,' she cried, 'since that I may choose and govern as I want?'

'Yes, certainly, my dear wife,' he replied, 'I think that is the best way.'

Kiss me,' she said. 'We will not quarrel anymore; for, on my word of honour, I will be both these things to you, that is to say, yea, both fair and good.

I prey to God that I moote sterven wood,
But I to yow be also good and trewe
As evere was wyf, sin that the world was newe.
And but I be to-morn as fair to seene
As any lady, emperice, or queene,
That is bitwixe the est and eke the west,
Dooth with my lyf and deth right as yow lest.
Cast up the curtin, looke how that it is.'
  And whan the knight saugh verraily al this,
That she so fair was, and so young therto,
For joye he hente hire in his armes two,
His herte bathed in a bath of blisse.

A thousand time a-rewe he gan hire kisse,
And she obeyed him in every thing
That mighte doon him plesance or liking.
  And thus they live unto hir lives ende
In parfit joye; and Jhesu Crist us sende
Housbondes meeke, yonge, and fressh abedde,
And grace t'overbide hem that we wedde;
And eek I praye Jhesu shorte hir lives
That wol nat be governed by hir wives;
And olde and angry nigardes of dispence,
God sende hem soone verray pestilence!

I pray God that I may die of madness, if I am not as good and true to you as ever wife was since the world began. And if I am not as beautiful to look at tomorrow, as any lady, empress or queen, between the east and the west, do with my life and death just what you will. Cast up the curtain, and see how it is.'

And when the Knight really saw this come to pass, that she was now so beautiful and so young, for sheer joy he seized her in his two arms, his heart swimming in a bath of bliss.

He kissed her a thousand times in a row, and she succumbed to him in everything that would give him pleasure and satisfaction.

And thus they lived to the end of their lives in perfect joy; and may Jesus Christ send us husbands who are meek, young and good in bed, and the grace to outlast those that we wed; and also I pray that Jesus may shorten the lives of those who will not be governed by their wives; and as for the old and angry misers of money, may God send them soon the very pestilence.

Textual notes

The Portrait of the Wife of Bath from the General Prologue, lines 445–76

445 **Bisyde Bathe** This is thought to refer to the parish of 'St Michael's Juxta Bathon', a parish of Bath where the weaving trade was concentrated. This is a singularly precise statement of locality and has led some scholars to argue that the character of the Wife of Bath was drawn from real life. Manly notes that the name 'Alisoun' (the Wife's Christian name) frequently occurs in the records of Bath in the fourteenth century.

446 **she was som-del deef** She lost her hearing in one ear as a result of a blow she received from her fourth husband for tearing out some pages in his book (Wife's Prologue, line 668).

447–8 The neighbourhood of Bath, particularly St Michael's parish (see note line 445 above), was well known for the manufacture of cloth. Ypres and Ghent were the main towns of the Flemish wool trade. Many Flemish weavers came to England in the fourteenth century bringing with them a high reputation for cloth-making. England was the main supplier of wool for the continent, and one of the causes of The Hundred Years War was the economic need to keep open the market for wool and cloth to Flanders.

449–52 **offrynge** The offertory was part of the service of mass during which 'offerings', that is gifts such as bread and wine, were made. The people went up to make their offerings in an accepted order of precedence, and the Wife of Bath, being a rich and 'worthy womman' (line 459), would consider that, in the absence of any nobility, she should have the first place among the women of the parish. Later we learn from the Wife's Prologue that her behaviour described here is very much in keeping with her character.

453–4 **coverchiefs** Kerchief or type of head-scarf. The simplicity that was in fashion during the thirteenth century gave way in the fourteenth century to richness and elaboration, and particularly in head-dress where the 'coverchief' was often fashioned in extravagant form and proportion. The coverchiefs were supported by wires to give the heavy complicated structures represented in medieval paintings and sculptures. It has been noted that the coverchief, as such, had not been 'in fashion' since the middle of the fourteenth century, but the Wife of Bath would be somewhat out-of-date anyway, living as she did in far-away Bath.

ful fyne were of ground Of very fine texture. Whether fashionable or not, the Wife's clothing was of very good quality.

456–7 **Hir hosen** The cloth or linen stockings which were short and gartered below the knee.

shoes ful moyste and newe The most expensive shoes were hand made and of soft supple leather.

458 **fair** Comely, attractive; nothing to do with colouring.

460 **Housbondes at Chirche dore** In medieval times the marriage ceremony was performed at the door of the Church, to be followed sometimes by a service inside. For those of high rank the marriage ceremony was performed inside the Church before the altar.

463–7 The Wife of Bath was much travelled: 'She coude muchel of wandrynge by the weye' (line 467). In the later Middle Ages the pilgrimage had become to many people something like the modern equivalent of a 'package holiday', with lodgings organized along the way and guided tours of the shrines. It was also a convenient and safe way for anyone who wanted to travel for pleasure, at home or abroad. The list of places visited by the Wife includes many of the most notable shrines in Europe. Jerusalem and Rome were obviously the main centres for pilgrimages.

Boloigne Boulogne contained a famous shrine of the Blessed Virgin.

In Galice at Seint Jame Santiago in Galicia (Spain), referring to the famous shrine of St James of Compostella.

Coloigne Cologne was the shrine of The Three Kings or Magi.

468 **Gat-tothed** Her teeth were set wide apart. This feature appears to have much significance. The Wife herself connects the feature with her amorous nature (Wife's Prologue, line 603). On the other hand, it was a mark of the influence of Mars at the time of her birth (Prologue, line 619) which bestowed on her, inter alia, the bold and unattractive qualities.

472 **foot mantel** It is not clear what this refers to. It would normally refer to a saddle cloth, but in this context probably means a blanket or outer skirt to keep her warm and clean whilst riding.

475 **remedyes of love** The charms, advice and tricks to secure the love of a person.

The Wife of Bath's Prologue

1 **auctoritee** Authoritative texts, the works and quotations from 'accepted' authorities, mainly ecclesiastical and classical writers.

4 Child marriages were not unusual in the Middle Ages. If this fact is taken in conjunction with the statement in the Portrait in the *General Prologue*, that she had had five husbands 'withooten sother

compaignye in youthe', we must assume that either there is boastful exaggeration or that the reference in the *General Prologue* refers to extra-marital relationships during the earlier marriages.

6 **Housbondes at chirche dore** See note to Portrait in *General Prologue*, line 460. In medieval times the marriage ceremony was performed at the door of the church.

7 **If I . . . ywedded be** That is if my several marriages are all considered to be valid. The medieval church argued that second marriages were not acceptable in the eyes of God, and emphasized the blessedness of permanent chastity in widowhood.

11 **Cane of Galilee** Cana in Galilee. This is a reference to St John's Gospel, 2, 1: 'There was a wedding in Cana-in-Galilee. The mother of Jesus was there, and Jesus and his disciples were guests also.'

13 **That I ne . . . but ones** That I should be married only once.

15–19 This is a reference to John, 4, 6, and the story of the Samaritan woman Jesus met on his journey to Galilee, while resting at a spring called Jacob's Well, near the Samaritan town of Sychar. In his effort to convert the Samaritan woman, Jesus tells her to go and fetch her husband, and she replied that she has no husband. 'You are right,' said Jesus, 'in saying that you have no husband, for although you have five husbands, the man with whom you are living is not your husband.'

23 In the eyes of the medieval church marriage was sacred, and a woman was allowed to marry only once: any subsequent marriage was considered to be bigamous. The Wife is questioning where this canon law is supported by Biblical authority.

25 **nombre diffinicioun** i.e. a precise number put on it.

28 A reference to Genesis, 1, 28: 'God blessed them and said to them "Be fruitful and multiply . . ." '

30–33 **he seyde** This would appear to follow on from the reference to God in Genesis as noted above for line 28. In fact the real source of lines 30–31 is the answer Jesus gave to the Pharisees in Judaea (Matthew 19, 5) when they asked him whether it was lawful for a man to divorce his wife. Jesus answered, 'In the beginning God made man and woman. For this reason a man shall leave his father and mother, and be made one with his wife; and the two shall become one flesh.' The Wife is quite correct, Jesus was making a comment on divorce, not about the unlawfulness of marrying again after the death of a husband. The churchman took this passage to confirm the sanctity of marriage and, incorrectly as the wife points out, the disallowance of subsequent remarrying.

bigamie The medieval church considered that remarriage, even after the death of a husband, was bigamous.

octogamie Octogamy, i.e. marrying eight times. This is taken from St Jerome.

34 **vileynie** Wrongdoing, not our meaning of villainy. Villeins were the labouring classes in feudal times, legally bound to the lord of the manor. With the economic and social upheaval during The Hundred Years War, and following The Black Death, there was much social discontent and many villeins left the serfdom of the manor to become poachers and outlaws (Robin Hood and his Merry Men).

35 **daun Salomon** Solomon, King of Judah, 'whose wisdom surpassed that of all men'. The reference here is to Kings 1, 11: 'King Solomon was a lover of women . . . He had seven hundred wives and three hundred concubines.'

daun Dan, a corruption of Latin 'dominus' meaning Master, a title given to persons holding a university degree, later used as a term of respect. It is the former equivalent of 'Mr'.

46–50 This reference is to the First Epistle of Paul to the Corinthians 7, 9: 'To the unmarried and widows I say this: it is a good thing that they stay as I am myself (i.e. chaste); but if they cannot control themselves, they should marry.'

th'apostle St Paul.

51–2 Again from the Corinthians. 'A wife is bound to her husband as long as he lives. But if the husband die, she is free to marry whom she will, provided the marriage is in the Lord's fellowship ('som Cristen man'); and, 'Better to be married than burn with vain desire.'

53 **seye vileynie:** Speak ill of. See note, line 34.

54 **shrewd Lameth and his bigamie** St Jerome quotes this reference to Genesis 4, 23: 'Lameth married two wives.' But Lameth married two wives at the same time, and therefore bigamously. Many of these allusions are taken from St Jerome's 'Epistola Adversus Jovinianum'. St Jerome was among the most famous of the early Biblical scholars. He preached asceticism and in his letter against Jovinian he commented adversely on marriage and upheld the superiority of the state of virginity.

63 **it is no drede** There is no fear of it (that is, contradiction).

64 **Th'apostel** Still referring to St Paul.

65 This refers to 1 Corinthians 7 where St Paul states quite openly: 'on the question of celibacy, I have no instructions (sic. 'precept') from the Lord.'

66 **to been oon** To be one of them, i.e. virgins.

68 **He putte it in oure owene juggement** Paul's message was: 'be celibate if you can, but if you do marry, there is nothing wrong in it.'

70 **With the dede** By that act, i.e. by commanding celibacy.

73 St Paul.

75–6 **The dart is set up** The dart or spear, apparently the prize for winning a contest – in this case the contest for celibacy. It may be that this refers to 1 Corinthians 9: 'You know that at the sports all the runners run the race, though only one wins the prize'.

Cacche whoso may i.e. Catch it whoever can, let's see who wins the race.

79 **th'apostel was a maide** St Paul was unmarried.

81 **swich as he** 1 Corinthians 7, St Paul says: 'To the unmarried and the widows I say this: it is a good thing if they stay as I am myself.'

83–4 **to been a wyf** In the same chapter in Corinthians St Paul says: 'but because there is so much immorality, let each man have his own wife, and each woman her own husband . . . All this I say by way of concession, not command.'

so nis it no repreve It is no shame. The double negative is used for emphasis, therefore the meaning is more 'there is absolutely no shame'.

85 **make** Match, mate.

87 Once again referring to St Paul (1 Corinthians, 7): 'It is a good thing for a man to have nothing to do with a woman.'

89 A homely proverb: it is dangerous to bring together fire and flax.

90 **ensample** Illustration, reference. You all know what this reference means.

92 **wedding in freletee** Marrying because the will is weak, i.e. lacking the strength of will to resist the temptations of the flesh.

95 **I graunte it wel** I accept it completely.

99–101 This reference is to the Epistle of Paul to Timothy (2.2.20): 'Now in any great house there are not only utensils of gold and silver, but also others of wood or earthenware.'

and doon hir lord servise And (yet) give their master good service.

103–4 **of God a propre yifte** Again from the Corinthians (1,7) 'but everyone has a gift God has granted him, one this gift and another that.'

as him liketh shifte As it pleases Him to provide.

107 **welle** The well or fountain-head.

116 **Were membres maad of generacion** For what purpose were the reproductive organs made. The Wife has developed her argument to its most logical conclusion. The case is unanswerable.

117 **wight** Normally means person. Here it is used diminutively, 'a little thing'.

124 **The experience** We know this from experience. The Wife's argument in her Prologue is to show that Experience is a better guide than Authority, and common-sense is a strong point in the Wife's favour.

127–8 **for office, and for ease/Of engendrure** For practical use and for sexual pleasure.

130 Another reference to St Paul (1 Corinthians, 7): 'Let each man have his own wife and each woman her own husband. The husband must give the wife what is due to her, and the wife equally must give the husband his due.' The Wife when drawing her support from the 'Authorities', emphasizes only those parts which suit her case, and conveniently omits those which embarrass her. In the *Prologue* she only emphasizes the obligations of the husband.

145–6 **Mark telle kan** The Wife gets her authority wrong here. It was John (John 6, 9), not Mark, who tells of the barley loaves in his account of the miracle of the loaves and the fishes, and the feeding of the five thousand.

147 **In swich estaat** 'Every man should remain in the condition in which he was called.' St Paul, 1 Corinthians, 7.

151 **If I be daungerous** i.e. if I should be grudging or stand-offish in any way. The meaning is that of 'difficult, off-hand, indifferent'. The word is not to be confused with our modern meaning. See also note line 1090. The word 'daunger' comes from the Old French 'dangier', itself derived from Latin 'dominus'. The original meaning was dominion, the power of lordship, and, therefore, the power to dispose of or harm. The modern meaning, 'liability to exposure of harm or injury, risk and peril', did not develop until late in the fifteenth century.

153 **paye his dette** See note line 130 above.

154–5 This is the prime ambition of the Wife of Bath, the underlying theme of her *Prologue* and the theme of her *Tale.* A husband should not only carry out his obligations, but be a servant to his wife, and this will avoid the '*wo that is in marriage*' of which St Paul warns, and to which the Wife refers in her opening remark.

An housbonde I wol have, I wol not lette Just in case her argument has not convinced the audience, the Wife in her typical determined and defiant way, states exactly what she wants, and what she is going to have.

158–9 The Wife (quite in character) distorts the message of St Paul not merely to advance her argument about the acceptance of 'authority' for marriage and its comforts, but also to establish an authority to support her concept of sovereignty in marriage (see note, line 130).

and noghte he In this the Wife is quite wrong, of course. St Paul clearly states that the husband is to enjoy the same rights as the wife: 'The wife cannot claim her body as her own; it is her husband's. Equally, the husband cannot claim his body as his own; it is his wife's.' (1 Corinthians, 7). The Wife knows this quite well, but it is in keeping with her character to distort and manipulate.

160–1 **the Apostel** Again St Paul, but this time the reference is to his Letter to the Ephesians, 5, 25: 'Husbands, love your wives, as Christ also loved the Church and gave himself up for it . . .' This exhortation is enough for the Wife to illustrate her point. It would not suit her purpose to quote the parallel exhortation in the same letter as well; 'Wives, be subject to your husbands as to the Lord; for the man is the head of the woman, just as Christ also is head of the Church.' These are examples of Chaucer's subtleness in dramatic irony. Chaucer's audience would have a very good idea of the teachings of St Paul, and would be very amused by this vital, clever yet wholly biased use of the Scriptures to support an argument.

162 Considering the biased use the Wife has made of St Paul's teaching, this self-satisfied remark illustrates the very essence of the Wife's engaging character and Chaucer's comic genius. It is also the most perfect ending to the first section of the Prologue, which purpose is to prove the importance of marriage. But with a subtle and clever twist, Chaucer makes the Wife touch on the subject of 'power' which will naturally lead to the next stage concerned with sovereignty in marriage.

163 **Pardoner** Pardoners were sellers of papal indulgences, and the abuses which they practised on the ignorant were condemned by both cleric and lay alike. Chaucer's Pardoner was an example of the worst kind (see *General Prologue,* lines 669 to 714), and Chaucer is not sparing in satire in describing his portrait.

167 **What sholde I bye it on my flessh so deere** Why should I bring such troubles on myself at such a high price? The use of 'what' as an interrogative is commonly used by Chaucer.

168 **no wyf to-yeere** No wife this year. To-yeere usually has the meaning 'this year', but it is likely that with the negative the meaning has more of the sense of 'never', or 'not at all'.

170 This is understood to be a colloquial expression. The meaning is 'you will drink another caskful of this draught (i.e. the tribulation in marriage) before I'm finished'.

172 **my tale** The tale, in fact, does not start until almost another 700 lines have passed! Clearly the Wife is referring to the 'story' of her husbands.

182–3 **Ptholomee** Ptolemy, a Greek astronomer, mathematician and geographer of the second century. His major work, the *Almagest,* is a complete textbook on Astrology, and became the authority on the subject, dominating astrological theory in the Arabic world from which it came to Europe in the Middle Ages. In fact, the title of the work, the *Almagest,* is a corruption of the Arabic 'al majisti'.

184 **Dame** i.e. Madam. The Wife would be pleased to be addressed as 'Madam', which was the title given to the wives of important officials and the upper classes. Compare the reference to the wives of the five

burgesses in the *General Prologue* (line 376): 'It is ful fair to been y-cleped "madame".' This approach is typical of the obsequious flattery of the Pardoner.

if youre wil it were If you would be so kind. The Pardoner is being very courteous and seems to be very keen that the Wife should continue with her illustrations of the *'wo that is in marriage'*. In other tales it is usually the Host who interrupts to push along the tale, but in this case the Pardoner, who has just revealed that he is contemplating marriage, has had his curiosity aroused.

187 **us yonge men** The Pardoner is one of the most unsavoury of the characters on the pilgrimage. He tries to hide his age and unpleasing appearance by treating his hair and dressing in the style of a young gallant. This is another example of Chaucer's use of the 'links' not only for a dramatic purpose but also to develop, by a touch here and a touch there, the character of each of the pilgrims. We see this again at the end of the *Prologue* in the sharp exchange between the Friar and the Summoner.

191–2 **taketh not agrief** Do not take amiss what I have to say. In the *Prologue to The Miller's Tale* Chaucer uses the same technique to apologize in advance for subject matter that might be distasteful to some of the audience. In fact, this technique is very clever, sharpening the interest in anticipation of what is to come. The unanswerable logic and bold frankness of the Wife's argument must have been dramatic enough for any medieval audiences. Now she tells that: 'my tale is nat bigonne', and there is a lot worse to come.

193 **I telle forth my tale** She keeps promising to come to her tale (see line 172) which does not, in fact, start until line 857.

198 **The statut holde** The obligation keep, i.e. the obligation set down by St Paul (see notes to line 130 and line 160 above).

204–8 This is an illustration of the unabashed materialistic outlook of the Wife.

217–18 **The bacon** The Dunmow Flitch. At Dunmow, near Chelmsford in Essex, a flitch or side of cured bacon was given (and still is to this day) to any married couple who had passed the year without quarrelling or wishing to be parted.

225 **Ye wise wives** The only female company on the pilgrimage are the Prioresse and another nun. But the word 'wyf' can also mean 'woman', and anyway the Wife of Bath is now in full flight, as it were, in her reminiscence.

226 **Bere him on honde** A colloquial expression meaning 'to deceive' or 'to put in the wrong'. Compare with lines 232 and 380.

232–4 **Bere him on Honde that the cow is wood** To deceive him that the chough is mad. This refers to a folk story of the 'Tell-tale Bird' where the bird (a chough) betrays to the husband an illicit love affair of the wife. The story tells of a wife who entertains her lover in the presence of a talking bird. When the husband returns home, the bird relates what it has seen. When accused by the husband of her infidelity, the wife denies the charge and protests that the bird is mad. To make her statement convincing, the wife, with the help of her maid, simulate the noise of a storm over the bird's cage during the night, and when the next morning the bird describes the storm during the night, the husband is convinced by his wife's statement that the bird is mad. A different version of the story is the subject of the *Manciple's Tale*.

235 et seq The material for the following tirade in which the Wife illustrates the way she scolded her husbands, is drawn from several sources which were well known in Chaucer's time, but mainly from the writings of St Jerome and Theophrastus (whom Jerome quotes). Refer to our notes on these anti-feminists in the section on *The Wife of Bath's Prologue*, and to the notes on lines 671–5.

247 **on thy bench** The bench and table were part of the usual furniture in medieval houses. A chair was rather a special item.

249 **for costage** Because of the cost, or expense. A poor woman naturally brought with her no dowry.

269–70 **Ne noon so grey goos** Apparently a proverbial saying, with the same meaning as 'Every Jack has his Jill'.

278–80 Another proverbial expression. Also used in Chaucer's story of the other pilgrims, *The Tale of Melibee.* In this tale, Dame Prudence, in a similar woman versus man debate, protests that: 'men seyn that thre thynges dryven a man out of his hous, that is to seyn, smoke, droppyng of reyn, and wikked wyves.' '*Tale of Melibee*, lines 1085 et seq.

283 **Til we be fast** Until we are secure, i.e. safe and married.

285–291 These lines are another illustration of Chaucer's borrowings from the anti-feminist literature of his time. This passage is part of the opinion of Theophrastus from his Liber Aureolus de Nuptiis which became known through quotations in the writings of St Jerome: 'Horses, asses, cattle, even slaves of the smallest worth, clothes, kettles, wooden seats, cups and earthenware pitchers, are first tried and then bought: a wife is the only thing that is not shown before she is married, for fear that she may not give satisfaction.' (Translation by N. H. Freemantle. *The Principal works of St Jerome*). See notes on line 54, line 235, lines 671–5.

303 **oure apprentice Jankin** Jankin appears again at line 595 as the young clerk who became her lover, and later her fifth husband. It seems that the suspicions of the husband are well founded.

307 **I wol him noght** I don't want him at all. This bold, blatant rejection of a suspicion which is quite clearly justified, and which is confirmed by later events, illustrates very well the confident, direct approach of this extraordinary character in the treatment of her husbands.

311 **oure dame** The mistress or lady of the house, i.e. myself.

312 **Seint Jame** St James of Compostella. St James was the first of the twelve disciples to suffer martyrdom being beheaded by Herod. According to old Spanish tradition, the body of St James was miraculously translated to Compostella, a city in Northwest Spain, properly Santiago (i.e. St James) de Compostella, where it was traditionally supposed that the body of the apostle was buried. The shrine of St James became a major centre for pilgrimage, and the Wife of Bath had visited the shrine among her many other travels. See *General prologue*, line 466.

320 **dame Alis** Alice. This is the first record of the Wife's Christian name. She is also referred to as Alison in line 804.

324–5 **The wise astrologien** Ptolemy. See note to line 35 and 182–3.

341–5 **wordes in the Apostles name** The reference is to the First Letter of Paul to Timothy, 2, 9: 'Women must dress in becoming manner, modestly and soberly, not with elaborate hair-styles, not decked out with gold or pearls, or expensive clothes, but with good deeds.'

356 **my borel** Coarse woollen clothes. Not the gayest clothing, but the Wife is being sarcastic, referring to her husband's pointed reference to the teaching of St Paul that women should dress modestly and not gaily. Lines 341–5 above.

358 **Argus** Argus, a monster in Greek mythology of huge strength and size, and a hundred eyes. The Wife is referring to the story of Io, a priestess of Hera, wife of Zeus. Zeus fell in love with Io and because of the suspicions of Hera, turned her into a white cow. Hera, still suspicious, claimed the cow as her own, and ordered Argus to keep watch with his hundred eyes. Zeus sent Hermes to steal Io back, but unable to pass undetected by one of Argus's hundred eyes, charmed him to sleep by playing the flute, then killed him and released Io.

361 **make his berd.** A colloquial expression meaning to 'outwit' or 'delude'; a phrase for cheating like 'pull him by the beard'. Compare the same expression in *The Reeve's Tale* 'Yet kan a millere make a clerkes berd'.

362–5 Borrowed from St Jerome, but the original source is thought to be Proverbs, 30: 'At three things the earth shakes, four things it cannot bear: a slave turned king, a churl gorging himself, a woman unloved when she is married.'

371–5 Also borrowed from St Jerome, and similarly thought to originate from Proverbs 30: 'Three things there are which will never be satisfied, four which never say 'Enough'! The grave and the barren womb, a land thirsty for water and fire that never says "Enough"!'

wild fyr A combination of highly inflammable materials that cannot be quenched with water.

383 **Janekin** Jankin has clearly a close relationship with the Wife. See lines 303 above and 595 following.

385 **Ful giltelees** The husbands were innocent of any misdemeanour. The Wife's technique is to 'bere him on honde' (lines 226 and 232) although all the time she was in the wrong (line 387).

389–90 Another frank confession by the Wife of how she managed to subdue her husbands.

401–2 These are some of the talents which according to the Wife give woman a superior wit over man.

414 **Winne** The old sense of 'win', i.e. gaining money, making profit.

415 A common proverb. No one can bring a hawk back with an empty hand. The proverb also appears in *The Reeve's Tale*: 'With empty hand men may nat haukes tulle.'

418 **bacon** Old meat.

436 **Jobes pacience** The patience of Job. Job, 'the greatest man in all the East', was allowed by God to be beset with calamities instigated by Satan, in order to test his faithfulness and loyalty. In spite of the destruction and ruin heaped on him, Job kept his faith with God and won through to be restored to his family and fortune.

446 **Peter** By St Peter.

455–6 This is a wonderful description of the Wife when she was young. The attributes are still there, though becoming dulled with age. See lines 474–6 below.

460 **Metellius** The story is told by the Roman historian Valerius Maximus. Maximus wrote a handbook on rhetoric that would have interested Chaucer, which he illustrated with stories.

464 **Venus** Venus, the planet which bestows amorousness, and in whose 'mansion' of Taurus the wife was born.

474–6 There is a pathos in this remark, particularly with reference to lines 455–6 above. But the Wife is under no illusion about her growing middle-age, and it is characteristic of her to shrug off the serious implications of age for a woman of her nature, with bold defiance.

483 **Seint Joce** Jodocus, a Breton Saint. This is a strange reference. Some Chaucer scholars think that Chaucer may have borrowed the reference from the *Roman de la Rose*.

487 A proverbial expression which we still use now, i.e. 'he stewed in his own juice'.

489–90 **in erthe I was his purgatorie** i.e. hell on earth. There are many medieval references, particularly amongst the anti-feminist literature, to both women and marriage being the equivalent of hell on earth. One particularly interesting parallel is quoted by Professor F. N. Robinson where God defends himself for having instituted matrimony as a purgatory on earth because it was not appropriate for him to desire the death of the sinful.

purgatorie Purgatory, a sort of middle ground between heaven and hell. In the Catholic doctrine, it is described as a state of existence or condition of the soul that has died in a state of grace, but has not been purified yet from all possible stain of unforgiven venial sins (minor or allowable sins), forgiven mortal sins, imperfections or evil habits.

his soule be in glorie i.e. in heaven. The unpurified souls had to pass through purgatory first for purification before being allowed to enter heaven.

492 A common expression, e.g. 'where the sole pinches'.

495 **I cam fro Jerusalem** Came back from Jerusalem, one of the pilgrimages mentioned in the *General prologue*, line 463.

496 **the roode beem** The timber beam, usually between the chancel and the nave of a parish church, on which was placed the crucifix (cross or rood). This indicates the relative importance of the person buried, the nearer the chancel the more important the person – and the more expensive the burial arrangements. The Wife did not consider her fourth husband too important (line 500), although she was prepared to take some trouble over the carving of his gravestone (lines 497–9).

498–9 **Darius** Darius I, the Great King of Persia (c. 500 BC) was one of the greatest rulers in ancient history, whose fame was widespread for his administrative genius and great building projects.

Appelles A Jewish craftsman who was said to be the sculptor of the legendary tomb of Darius.

514 **daungerous** Cool, indifferent. Very different from our present meaning. See note line 151 above.

516 **a queynte fantasie** Quaint or peculiar ideas on this matter. 'Queynte' has a range of meanings, both colourful and sexual, which defy accurate modern translation. Compare line 444 above.

521 **With daunger oute** When we meet with indifference, we bring out all the attractive wares. For the meaning of 'daunger' refer to the notes at lines 151 and 514 above.

522 A proverbial expression, i.e. a big crowd at the market pushes up the price of goods.

527 **a clerk of Oxenford** A student at the University of Oxford. 'Clerk' is nearer our meaning of 'cleric'. Students in Chaucer's day were 'church apprentices', destined for the church in one capacity or other. The clergy (i.e. the clerks) because they were almost the only educated class (meaning someone who could read and write) often undertook secretarial and administrative duties. We know that Jankin had previously been the secretary (line 303, 'our apprentice Janekin') to

one of the Wife's old rich husbands, who would have needed someone literate to keep his books.

528 **wente at hom to bord** Went to board at the house of her friend. Compare the old carpenter in *The Miller's Tale* who took in lodgers: 'A riche gnof, that gestes heeld to bord.' And one of his lodgers was Nicholas, the dynamic and clever 'clerk of Oxenford', the hero of *The Miller's Tale*. 'Bord is the board or table on which meals were served, cf 'board and lodging'.

530 **Alisoun** She had the same name as the wife. See lines 320 (Alis) and 804 (Alisoun).

532 The Wife as a regular church-goer (see *General Prologue,* the Wife's Portrait, line 450–2) would confess her sins to the parish priest, and no doubt she would have enjoyed the confession, for in the Middle Ages parish priests were instructed to hold confessions with women out in the open in the body of the church (the church had been very suspicious of women, and the temptations they brought, ever since the transgression of Eve) where everyone could see, though not, of course hear.

543 **Lente** Lent, period from Ash Wednesday in February to Easter, a period of forty days devoted to fasting and penitence in commemoration of Christ's period in the wilderness. The Wife does not observe the rules for penance and abstaining from festivities of any sort.

555–8 **visitaciouns** The Wife attended all the entertainments that were presented during the Saints' days, feast days and 'holy days'.

556 **vigilies** Vigils. These were religious services held on the eve of a Saint's day. It was usually an occasion for festivity and entertainment. Vigils are referred to in the *General Prologue* (l.377) in connection with the wives of the five guildsmen, who liked to be called 'madam', and take precedence when attending vigils, which implies that attending vigils was a social occasion.

processiouns On certain feast days, notably that of the Feast of Corpus Christi, processions were usual, varying in pomp and splendour according to the richness or otherwise of the town, in which the blessed sacrament was carried through the streets. These feast days and saints' days, or 'holy days', became associated with the performance of Mystery or Miracle Plays (line 558) presented by the craft guilds, and they in their turn became associated with the procession, drawing the moveable stages and pageants behind the religious vanguard, guild vying with guild as to the magnificence of pageantry. The event would be similar to the present day Lord Mayor's Show.

557 **To preching** Preaching was a popular form of entertainment in the Middle Ages, and normally took place in the open. The professional preachers, like the wandering Friars, drew large

audiences. The people were delighted to learn about stories from the Bible, for, being mostly illiterate, listening was their only means of learning.

pilgrimages Pilgrimages became very popular in the Middle Ages, for those who had a pious desire to visit shrines hallowed by tradition or like the Wife of Bath, just to travel and see the world. The most distant shrines (Jerusalem, Rome, Compostella, all of which the Wife had visited – *General Prologue.* Portrait of the Wife, see note lines 463–7) were naturally considered the most desirable.

558 **pleyes of miracles** The Miracle Plays were very popular in the fourteenth century and were usually organized by the town guilds during the religious festivals. They portrayed dramatic versions of Bible stories in an age when the Bible as a book was known to few people. Each body of guildsmen undertook to produce a single episode or scene, and great pride was taken in the production. The 'pageants' on which the plays were acted were large wooden structures mounted on four wheels. The simple audience demanded drama, humour and realism, and considerable trouble and ingenuity were taken to represent such scenes as 'Hell's Mouth' and 'Paradise', by means of canvas hangings or wooden structures garishly painted. The plays, of course, were a great social event.

558 **mariages** Marriages, then as now, were social events and opportunities for gossip and dressing-up.

572–4 The mouse with only one hole to escape to is proverbial.

575 **enchanted me** In the literal sense of 'bewitched', with undertones of magic and sorcery. Not the modern meaning.

576 **My dame** The reference is unclear, but it most likely means 'my mother' or 'my godmother'. The French literature of the time (from which Chaucer took many of his references), contains references to *la mère* (the mother).

581 **Blood bitokeneth gold** In the medieval interpretation of dreams, gold and blood have a relationship, each signifying the other.

590 **coverchief** Kerchief or type of head-scarf. See note to the Portrait of the Wife in the *General Prologue*, lines 453–4. The kerchief somewhat resembled a turban and some reports say that the kerchief was only worn by provincials in the fourteenth century.

595 **oure clerk** This confirms that Jankin had been employed as a secretary in the Wife of Bath's household.

597–8 **paire/Of legges** The style of dress was changing in Chaucer's time. The normal male dress was a long gown and plain hood. But Chaucer's fashionable contemporaries, particularly the younger men, abandoned the gown for a short coat or tunic, with buttons all down the front, in gay colours and fitting tightly. This would display the shape of the legs in the tight-fitting hose.

602 **a coltes tooth** A taste for frisky young activities. A common expression with a meaning associated with lusty animal behaviour. The expression, probably proverbial, occurs in the same context in *The Reeve*'s *Prologue*, when the Reeve bemoans his age and senility. He adds that, though the ability has gone, the desire remains: 'And yet ik have alwey a coltes tooth.'

603 **Gat-tothed** With teeth set wide apart (i.e. gap-toothed or gate-toothed). This feature is mentioned in the portrait of the Wife in the *General Prologue*. (See note on line 468 of the *General Prologue*). This feature appeared to be regarded in the Middle Ages as a sign that the possessor would be 'lucky and travel', which in part fits the Wife's description. Here, however, the Wife seems to consider the feature as a sign of her amorous nature. Chaucer perhaps drew on the interpretation of the medieval physiognomists who regarded the feature as a sign of boldness, falseness, gluttony and lasciviousness. This last interpretation appears to be more in keeping with the character of the Wife, from what we learn from her confessions, and from her horoscope (lines 609–20) as one of the influences of Mars.

604 **the prente of seinte Venus seel** The birthmark of Venus. The Wife considered that she was strongly subject to the influence of Venus (and Mars as well). The medieval astrologers believed that there were definite characteristics, and indeed physical marks, associated with the planets. People in the Middle Ages seriously believed that astrology had a very real influence on their lives, in fact so much so that it became inextricably mixed up with the Christian religion – hence 'Seinte Venus'.

606 The Wife still considered herself attractive, rich, young enough and well provided for, and therefore in every way a suitable wife for the best.

wel bigon Well provided for. Remember the Wife had already had three rich husbands who had bequeathed to her all their land and possessions (line 204).

609–20 **I am al Venerien** Astrology for most of Chaucer's contemporaries was a very real science, and was considered the major influence of a person's make-up and behaviour. The Wife herself blames her 'constellacioun' (meaning her horoscope or 'aspect' of the planets at the moment of her birth), for her nature. Like the signs of the Zodiac, each planet had its own attributes and influences. As far as the Wife of Bath is concerned there were two planetary associations, Venus and Mars, Venus, considered a lucky or fortunate planet, brought luck and amorousness. Mars was the planet of war, and association with Mars brought about an aggressive or martial temperament. The horoscope of the Wife (lines 609–16) tells us that she was born under Taurus, but in that sign at the time there were the two planets Venus and Mars. In such circumstances, Venus would take precedence because Taurus was one of her 'mansions'. Unfortunately,

Mars was also, at the time, in the ascendant in Taurus, thereby influencing and debasing the refining influence of Venus, and adding coarseness and strength. Thus there are two opposing and opposite influences affecting the character of the Wife – amorousness and pleasure-seeking corrupted by aggressiveness and 'sturdy hardiness'. For the influences of the planets on her character, refer to our notes in the section, The character of the Wife of Bath.

I am al Venerien The major influences come from Venus.

610–12 **In feelinge** i.e. outwardly and emotionally she had all the attributes of Venus, but inwardly, 'myn herte' she was the subject of Mars and inclined to be aggressive. In medieval astrology the heart was considered the source of vital spirits.

613 **Taur** Taurus, the Bull, one of the Twelve Signs of the Zodiac. Taurus gave her the bold, broad red face and a tendency towards affairs of the heart.

614 **that evere love was sinne** To make love with the sole object of enjoying oneself was considered by the church fathers to be a sin. The only acceptable reason for intercourse was for the purpose of procreation. The Wife is complaining that this doctrine has inhibited her from following to the full her Venusian influence. From her own account of her life and affairs, there appears to have been no such inhibition in her sexual behaviour.

sinne In the medieval church there were categories of sins with different orders of importance, from Venial, those which were excusable and pardonable, to Mortal, impardonable from any standpoint, e.g. murder. See notes on Purgatory, lines 489–90.

615–20 **I folwed ay myn inclinacioun** The Wife is excusing her excesses in love-making by blaming her behaviour on the unavoidable force (*vertu*) of her planetary influences (*constellacioun*). This would be an acceptable excuse as the influence of astrology was taken very seriously by medieval people.

618 **Chambre of Venus** There are two meanings implied – the influence of the 'mansion' of Venus, and the part of the body usually referred to as the 'queynte'.

619 **Martes Mark** i.e. the mark or attribute of Mars. The Wife's attributes were mainly conditioned by Venus, but Mars debased this influence so that her amorousness became coarse and lecherous. The outward mark of Mars would be her ruddy complexion and the gaps in her teeth.

620 The Wife possesses the birthmark of Venus (line 604). She may mean that she has another, the red birthmark of Mars, or just the 'sturdy hardiness' of certain parts of her body. (Lines encircling the woman's neck are sometimes called the 'rings of Venus'.)

630–2 This is the one mistake the Wife made, for which she sorely repented. This is the result of a middle-aged woman believing that she has fallen in love and, as a result, abandoning all the experience and business acumen she was so proud to advertise.

635 To tear a page out of a book might seem a small matter to us, but in Chaucer's time books were rare and expensive. It was some time before the invention of printing, and books had to be laboriously copied by hand from the original manuscript.

636 **myn ere wax al deef** The deafness of the Wife is the first feature mentioned in her portrait in the *General Prologue*, line 446.

638 **verray jangleresse** An incorrigible chatterbox and gossip. The same term is applied to the Miller in his portrait: 'He was a janglere and a goliardeys.'

642–3 **olde Romain geestes** Stories from Roman history. As with the reference at line 460, the reference here is to the stories in the work of the Roman historian Valerius Maximus. The story of Simplicius Gallus, and the story of 'another Romain' (line 647) are taken from the same chapter in Maximus's book.

648 **Someres game** Summer party, summer festival. Some scholars see a reference to a Midsummer festival of pagan origin, or Roman Saturnalia, which activities attracted moral censure.

651 **ilke proverbs of Ecclesiaste** Referring to Ecclesiasticus 25, 34 (in the Roman Catholic Douai Bible):

Do not leave a leaky cistern to drip, or allow a bad wife to do what she likes.

655 This is a proverbial expression.

657 **seken halwes** Seek hallowed places, i.e. to go looking for shrines and relics – to go on pilgrimages.

659 **an hawe** Hawthorn, used as a symbol of worthlessness.

666 **Seint Thomas** Thomas à Becket whose shrine at Canterbury was the objective of the Canterbury pilgrims. Thomas à Becket, Archbishop of Canterbury in the reign of Henry II, met a martyr's death in Canterbury Cathedral some two hundred years before Chaucer's day, in 1107. Becket had taken sanctuary in the Cathedral where he was killed by four knights (on the orders of the king), thus making the death a martyrdom. Becket became a saint soon after his martyrdom because of supposed curative powers thought to be in his miraculously preserved blood. In Chaucer's day, the pilgrimage to St Thomas's shrine was claimed to bring many other blessings besides the healing of ailments.

671–5 The works first mentioned that were included in Jankin's book, Valerius, Theophrastus and St. Jerome, are three Latin anti-feminist treatises from which Chaucer draws much of his material for the *Wife of Bath's Prologue*.

671 **Valerie** Epistola Valerii ad Rufinum de non Ducenda Uxore, or The Letter from Valerius to Rufinus about not controlling a wife. This was the work of Walter Map, a twelfth century churchman and canon of Lincoln Cathedral, who was a theological scholar, and a cynical and dedicated anti-feminist.

Theofraste Theophrastus c. 372 BC, a Greek philosopher and pupil of Aristotle. The work referred to is *Liber Aureolus de Nuptiis*, a book about marriage which was known through quotation from the writings of St Jerome, another dedicated anti-feminist.

674 **Seint Jerome** The major source of Chaucer material. St Jerome was an Italian priest and scholar who lived in the late fourth and early fifth centuries. He was thought to have been a cardinal, but there is no evidence for this; he did, however, become Secretary to the Pope. Jerome's scholarship was unsurpassed in the early church. His greatest achievement was the translation of most of the Bible into Latin from Hebrew. His correspondence was of great interest and historical importance. He preached extreme asceticism.

675 **again Jovinian** This refers to St Jerome's Letter to Jovinian, the Epistola Adverus Jovinianum. Jovinian was a fifth century monk, whose unorthodoxy was condemned by the Synods of Rome. He denied that virginity as such was a superior state to marriage, or that abstinence as such was better than thankful eating. It is understandable that such radical and heretical views were attacked so vigorously by such stalwarts of orthodoxy at St Jerome.

676 **Tertulan** Tertullian, an early Roman Christian and theologian. He was a well known apologist for orthodox Christianity and an essayist on Christian morals. He had a great power for invective, and sarcasm was one of his favourite weapons. In one of his works, De Monogamia, he stigmatizes all second marriages as adultery.

677 **Crisippus** Scholars think that this reference is to the person mentioned by St Jerome, Chrysippus, whom he considered stupid to instruct a wise man to take a wife so as not to offend the gods.

Trotula Trotula is thought to refer to a well known female doctor or midwife from Salerno in Southern Italy, who lived about the middle of the eleventh century. She was known for her writings on, inter alia, the diseases of women.

677–8 **Helowis** Heloise, the secret wife of the monk Abelard and later prioress of a convent near Paris. This story of Heloise and Abelard is famous in the history of literature. Abelard, a monk, was a famous twelfth century French philosopher. He was made tutor to the young Heloise, the niece of the Canon of Notre Dame. They fell in love, and Abelard carried her off to Brittany to marry her secretly. Heloise returned to Paris and her uncle for the sake of Abelard's career. Heloise took the veil, and Abelard became a monk. When they died, they were buried together.

679 **Parables of Salomon** The Book of Proverbs.

680 **Ovides Art** Ovid's *Ars Amatoria*. Ovid was one of the greatest poets of classical Rome and his works had a primary influence on European literature. Ovid was the arch-poet of love, a theme that in his work achieved a new range and significance. The *Ars Amatoria* is a handbook on the subject of love, a work of polished cynicism describing the gay, decadent, pleasure-loving society of Augustan Rome, in which Ovid included tales of myth and legend to illustrate his argument.

685 **book of wikked wives** 'Wife' was also used as a term for 'woman'. Certainly the writers mentioned were not protagonists of the female sex.

686 **legendes and lives** Stories and biographies. Normally used with reference to the lives of saints. An ironic comment.

689 **clerk** That is, scholar or the 'auctoritee' with whose writings the Wife was in conflict. (See note, line 527.) The Wife is referring to the scholars' antagonism to women. The scholars of the church took their lead from the Book of Genesis, which proclaimed woman's inferiority and traced the historical origin of sin to the transgression of Eve.

692 **Who peyntede the leon** This reference is not easily understood. Scholars see an allusion here to *Aesop's Fables*. Skeat prefers the fable in Aesop where a sculptor represented a man conquering a lion. The lion replied that he knew of cases in which the lion conquered the man. The moral does suit the Wife's comment in lines 693–6. Robinson refers to another of Aesop's fables, 'The Man and the Lion'. In the fable a rich man dreamed that a lion would kill his only son, who was a great hunter. To avoid this, he had built a special house, in which the son was made to live for his safety. The house was full of paintings, among which was a painting of a lion. The son became frustrated by his incarceration, and in a fit of temper smashed his fist into the painting of the lion, injuring his hand on a nail in the wall. The injury became poisoned and the young son died. There are many variants of Aesop's fables, having been transmitted by word of mouth until they were documented in the fourteenth century by a monk called Maximus Planudes.

694 **hire oratories** An oratory was a chapel or closet for private meditation or devotion. The Wife's point is what do these celibate scholars, who scribble away in their little cells far removed from the reality of the world, know about the activities of woman.

696 All those with the likeness of Adam, i.e all men.

697–700 **The children of Mercurie and of Venus** Those who are born under the influence of the planets Mercury and Venus. Mercury is a changeable planet, and his influence varies according to his conjunction with other planets. He is mainly associated with learning, making men studious and seekers after knowledge. Mercury is, therefore, associated with the '*clerkes*', and it is not surprising that the

Wife comments on the conflict between Mercury and her planet Venus (see notes, lines 609–14), '*Been in hir wirking ful contrarius*'.

701–5 According to medieval astrology, the 'exaltation' of one planet, that is the Sign of the Zodiac in which its influence is greatest, is the 'defection' or 'desolation' (*desolat*) of another planet of contrary nature (*diverse disposicioun*). Thus the Zodiacal Sign of Pisces is the 'exaltation' of Venus, and the 'defection' of Mercury. The reason for the conflict between the Venusian Wife of Bath and the Mercurial 'authorities' is both natural and precisely explained.

715–20 **Eva** Eve, whose sin it was to eat the forbidden fruit in the Garden of Eden, causing man to fall from grace – the origin of sin and all the subsequent troubles of mankind; later to be redeemed by Jesus, who gave his life to save mankind. The transgression of Eve was at the root of ecclesiastical anti-feminist thinking.

721 **Sampson loste his heres** This is a reference to the story of Samson and Delilah as described in the Book of Judges (14, 17). Samson was an Israelite who by his enormous strength, and the support of God, became the terror of the Philistines who were then masters of Israel. He felt in love with Delilah, who was bribed by the Philistines to discover the secret of Samson's great strength. Samson revealed to her that his strength was derived from his long hair. When he was asleep she caused his hair to be cut off and, having thus drained him of his strength, she betrayed him to the waiting Philistines, who gouged out his eyes and brought him in chains to Gaza. Delilah's name has since become synonymous with voluptuous and treacherous women.

725–6 **Hercules and of his Dianire** Deianeira gave her husband Hercules a poisoned tunic, and to escape the agony Hercules made his friends burn him alive. Whilst accompanying Hercules on a journey, Deianeira was ravished by the Centaur Nessus. On learning this, Hercules struck the centaur a mortal blow. As he was dying, Nessus gave Deianeira a potion made of his blood, claiming that an application would ensure Hercules' love for her. Deianeira forgot about the potion until she learned that Hercules had fallen in love with Iole. When Hercules called for fresh clothes, Deianeira spread the potion on a tunic and sent it to him, quite unaware that the centaur's blood contained the deadly poison of Hydra. When he put on the tunic, Hercules was afflicted by the poison, which burned his flesh and caused a terrible pain that could not be assuaged. Hercules ordered a funeral pyre to be made and, setting himself on it, was burnt to death. On learning of her husband's death and its cause, Deianeira killed herself.

728 **Socrates** The philosopher of Ancient Greece, who lived in the fifth century BC. He was the first of the great Greek philosophers, the others being Plato and Aristotle, who laid the philosophical foundations of Western culture.

729 **Xantippa** Xanthippe. Socrates married Xanthippe apparently late

in life. Socrates' friends speak of her high temper, giving the impression that she was a shrew.

733–6 **Phasipha** Pasiphae, wife of King Minos of Crete. When Minos offended the god Poseidon by refusing to sacrifice his most handsome bull, the god caused Pasiphae, his wife, to fall in love with a bull. As a result she gave birth to the Minotaur, half-man and half-beast, which Minos imprisoned in the famous Labyrinth.

737–8 **Of Clitermystra** Clytemnestra, wife of King Agamemnon who was the brother of King Menelaus, husband of Helen of Troy. When Paris, the son of Priam of Troy, abducted Helen, and thus provoked the Trojan War, both Agamemnon and Menelaus were absent from home for ten years. Aegisthus, a family enemy, for revenge planned not only to become Clytemnestra's lover, but also to kill Agamemnon when he returned from Troy. Clytemnestra herself had small cause to love Agamemnon. After killing her former husband, and the child at her breast, he had married her by force and then disappeared to a war that promised never to end. He had also caused her daughter Iphigenia to be sacrificed at Aulis, so as to bring good weather for the ships sailing for Troy. And – this she found even harder to bear – she had heard that, when he returned, Agamemnon would bring back Priam's daughter Cassandra as his wife. Clytemnestra therefore conspired with Aegisthus to kill Agamemnon on his return. When eventually Agamemnon came home, Clytemnestra persuaded him to bathe himself before dinner; and while he was in the bath she threw over him a net; and, thus entangled. Agamemnon perished by the sword of Aegisthus. Not satisfied, Clytemnestra avenged herself by beheading her dead husband with an axe.

741–6 **Amphiorax . . . Eriphilem** Amphiarus, an Argive nobleman was married to Eriphyle, the sister of Adrastus, King of Argus. Adrastus had promised to restore Polyneices to his rightful inheritance as ruler of Thebes, and to this end summoned the Argive chieftains, including Amphiarus, to march against Thebes. Amphiarus was reluctant, foreseeing that six of the seven chiefs, including himself, would be killed in the attack. Polyneices offered Eriphyle the magic necklace giving eternal beauty which had been Aphrodite's wedding gift to his ancestress Harmonia, if she would persuade her husband to join the expedition. This she did, and the Seven marched against Thebes. The attack was unsuccessful and, as Amphiarus had prophesied, all the chieftains were killed, except Adrastus.

747–56 **Livia** Livilla, wife of Drusus, who was persuaded by her lover, Sejanus, to poison her husband.

Lucie Lucilia, wife of the Greek poet Lucretius. Lucretius became so absorbed in his work that he had little time to entertain his wife. To encourage his love for her, Lucilia gave him a love potion which was so strong that it poisoned him.

757–64 **Latumius** The story of Latumius is told by Walter Map as ad quotation from Valerius's letter to Rufinus (Epistola Valerii ad Rufinum de non Ducenda Uxore. See note line 671). The story of the 'hanging tree' is told in many forms, and is an example of Map's cynical anti-feminist attitude.

769–70 **drive nailes in hir brain** This is probably a reference to the story of Jael and Sisera which is described in the Book of Judges, 4. After the Israelites had defeated the Canaanites, the defeated commander Sisera fled and found refuge in the tent of Jael who, when he was asleep, drove a tent-peg into his skull.

755–6 This is another of the obscure quotations which could be proverbial, or a variation of a Biblical quotation. Some scholars think that it could be a reference to Ecclesiasticus 25, 23: 'I would sooner share a home with a lion or a snake than keep house with a spiteful woman.'

778–9 This is clearly a reference to Proverbs 21: 'Better to live in a corner of a house-top than to have a nagging wife and a brawling household.'

784–5 Another quotation from Proverbs (11, 22): 'Like a gold ring in a pig's snout is a beautiful woman without good sense.'

813–15 **He yaf me at the bridel in myn hond** The Wife has regained that sovereignty in marriage which is the most important part of her philosophy of life, the main theme of her discourse and the theme of her *Tale*.

816 The burning of the cursed book was a symbolic act. This was not only the end of the influence of the 'authorities' with all their malicious anti-feminist propaganda, and with the scholarly approach which so antagonized the Wife, but it was also the reversal of the 'dominant force' – the 'defection' of Mercury with its seriousness, lack of humour and study of the ancients, and the 'exaltation' of Venus and the good life. See notes to lines 691–706.

818 **By maistrie** By mastery, with all the overtones of superior wit and skill.

820–5 These are very much the same arrangements which bring about the happy ending in the *Wife's Tale*.

And thus they live unto hir lives ende
In parfit joye.

829 **The Frere lough** The interest is now returned to the group of pilgrims, the 'link' which formed the dramatic interlude between the tales, giving coherence to the frame-work of the pilgrimage, adding human interest and additional touches of character make-up and preparing the ground for the next tale.

833 **Goddes armes two** This vulgar oath is in keeping with the

character of the Summoner who, with the Pardoner, make up the least attractive characters of the pilgrims.

834–9 The tone of these remarks illustrates how well Chaucer dramatically introduces a relationship between the Friar and the Summoner which heightens the anticipation to hear their tales.

837 **preambulacioun** One of the characteristics of the Summoner in his limited education (General Prologue, lines 638–45), and this is shown by his use of Latin phrases without any clear idea of their meaning. The Friar, who would have been relatively well educated, would be quick to spot this weakness.

842 **Telle of a somonour swich a tale or two** Which is exactly what the Friar does when his turn comes, and a slanderous tale about an association between a summoner and the Devil: in fact, so slanderous that the Summoner shakes with rage '*lyk an aspen leef*'. In the *General Prologue* it is stated that each pilgrim would tell two tales on the way to Canterbury, and two more tales on the journey home. This is confirmed by the remark of the Friar.

846 The Summoner has his turn later by telling an equally scandalous tale about a dishonest mendicant friar.

847 **Sidingborne** Sittingbourne in Kent, some 64 km (40 miles) from London, on the road to Canterbury.

850 **Oure Hooste** Harry Bailly, the landlord of the Tabard Inn who acted as host to the pilgrims on their journey to Canterbury, having been elected as leader of the party and organizer of the story-telling.

The Wife of Bath's Tale

857 King Arthour King Arthur the legendary British king who appears in a cycle of medieval romances as the leader and founder of the Knights of the Round Table. Early Celtic literature portrayed Arthur as a king of wonder and marvels. The history of Britain's legendary kings which was written by Geoffrey of Monmouth in the twelfth century marked the beginning of the Arthurian legend in the Middle Ages, when the Celtic stories of Arthur were adapted to suit a feudal background, but still retained the Celtic influences of magic and marvels.

858 **Britons** The ancient British people, the Celtic races of what are now Wales, Scotland, Ireland, Cornwall, the Isle of Man, and Britanny.

866 **Of limitours** 'Limiters', i.e. friars who had an exclusive right to beg in a prescribed (limited) area or district. Of the four Orders of Friars, two were not confined to monasteries – the Franciscans (or Grey Friars) and the Dominicans (or Black Friars). The founders of these orders wanted their friars to set an example of apostolic poverty, and

to direct themselves towards preaching and teaching, making their way by begging for a living – hence the term 'Mendicant Friars'. The mendicant friars exercised all the functions of the parish priest, which made them unpopular with the clergy, but they were welcomed by the people from whom they begged a living, not only for their 'stories', biblical or otherwise, but also for the 'news' they brought with them. The medieval friars were organized into groups, each friar being allocated a special area in which to preach and beg – 'limitacioun'. Chaucer's Friar was not a good example of the founder's ideal (*General Prologue*, lines 240–56), being corrupt and concerned only with the good things in life – 'the beste beggere in his hous'. He was probably a Franciscan, because the Summoner's Tale is about a dishonest mendicant friar who was of this Order. The Wife of Bath clearly does not like the Friar, or his trade.

867 **serchen** Literally, search, but also visit, haunt. All three meanings are implied. Chaucer's Friar would indeed 'search' for the best places offering comfort, including bedrooms and kitchens, (line 869).

869 **Blessinge** Making the sign of the cross to ward off evil spirits.

880 **Incubus** This is a reference to folk-tales of elves spiriting away young women. The 'incubus' was a supernatural male spirit (elf) who was supposed to have sexual intercourse with sleeping women, which always resulted in the woman conceiving a child. The Wife is referring to the fairy lover of the folk-tales, but is slanting her meaning to the amorous activities of friars in general, and to the Friar in particular.

883 **bacheler** A probationer for the honour of knighthood. The Squire in the *General Prologue* is described as 'a lovyere and a lusty bacheler'. The eldest son of a knight was a squire by birth. After a period of training, he would accompany his father or another knight on a campaign to continue his training and complete his probation.

904 The asking of a question, the answer to which means life or death, was a common theme in medieval tales of romance. By a clever arrangement of his source material, Chaucer has introduced the 'life-question' in a dramatic way to suit both the story and the purpose of the tale as an exemplum to the Wife's Prologue.

924 **according in-feere** Literally, agreeing together.

925–34 Compare Wife's Prologue lines 257–61 and *The Miller's Tale* (lines 273–4):

'For som folk wol ben wonnen for richesse.
And some for strokes, and some for gentillesse.'

938 **no thing nice** In no way foolish. The meaning of '*nice*' in Chaucer's time was very different from the meaning we give to the word today. It is one of those words, like 'clever', where the meaning has changed quite radically over the centuries, '*Nice*' comes from the French of the

same spelling, which was derived from the Latin word 'nescius' (nescire, to not know) meaning 'ignorant, foolish'; and it is used in the original meaning in this context. Chaucer also used the word with shades of 'fastidiousness, punctiliousness', but it still retained its essential meaning of 'foolishness' up to the early seventeenth century. From then on the meaning changed from 'fastidious' to 'precise' (the Battle of Waterloo was described by the Duke of Wellington as 'a damned nice thing'), and then to the modern sense of 'agreeable, kind, pleasant'.

940 **clawe us on the galle** Scratches us on a sore spot, i.e rubs us up the wrong way. The phrase was proverbial.

949 **nat worth a rake-stele** Literally, not worth a rake handle. This domestic image is typical of the Wife in her expression of scorn for something which cannot be considered reasonable. She herself was accustomed to tell all her most intimate secrets to her friend and gossip, Alisoun (lines 538–42).

951 **Mida . . . asses eres** Midas is best known for his gift for turning everything he touched to gold – The Midas Touch. This gift was bestowed on him by Bacchus for returning Silenus, Bacchus' tutor, who had been captured by a band of peasants. The 'ass's ears' comes from a subsequent story in Ovid's Metamorphoses. Pan challenged Apollo, the god of music, to a contest to see who could play the most enchanting music. Not suprisingly, Apollo was adjudged the winner, but Midas, who worshipped Pan, objected to the judgement, having been charmed by Pan's pipe music. For his temerity, and as a punishment for his 'bad ear for music', Apollo changed Midas' ears into ass's ears.

952 **Ovide** Ovid, one of the greatest poets in classical Rome, and the arch-poet of Love. Reference has already been made in the Wife's *Prologue* to Ovid's 'Ars Amatoria' ('Ovides Art' at line 680). The reference here, '*amonges othere thinges smale*', is to his masterpiece, the Metamorphoses, a collection of tales of classical myth and legend with the theme of transformation.

953–6 **Mida** Midas. See note above, line 951.

957–82 **save his wyf** In Ovid's tale Midas was so ashamed of his disfigurement that he concealed his ears by wrapping his head in a sort of turban. It was his barber, not his wife, who learned the secret, and not daring to reveal such a shameful thing, and yet not being able to keep quiet about it, dug a hole in the ground, whispered the secret into it, and filled the hole up again. However, the reeds which grew on the ground over the hole revealed the secret. When the wind blew through them they sang, 'King Midas has asses' ears'. The corruption of the tale to suit her own purpose is typical of the way the Wife treats her 'authorities'. On the other hand, the Wife might have got the modified version from her fifth husband, Jankin the 'clerk', and is merely repeating it innocently.

972 **as a bitore bombleth in the mire** Just as a bittern 'booms' in the mud. A bittern is marshland bird, and the song of the male is known as 'booming' or 'bellowing'.

983 **specially** Particularly concerned with.

991–2 **daunce** The ladies are presumably dancing in a 'fairy ring', a common activity in Celtic folk-tales.

1004 **Thise olde folk kan muchel thing** We old ones know a thing or two. This was a proverbial saying.

1009 **Plight me thy trouthe heere in myn hand** The troth, or promise, is plighted by joining hands, e.g. 'shaking hands on the agreement'.

1018 **coverchief or a calle** Head-dress. See note line 590.

1025 **as he sayde** As he had tried (to find out), i.e. to the best of his ability, '*sayde*' is from '*sayen*', meaning 'to try, endeavour'; and not from '*sayen*' 'to say, speak', as in the previous line '*seyde*'.

1027 **widwe, for that they been wise** Another of the Wife's 'throwaway remarks' of which she is so fond, and which support the good impression she has of herself.

1028 **The queene hirself sittinge as a justice** i.e. as the presiding judge of the court.

1038–40 **sovereinetee** The prime objective of the Wife of Bath.

maistrie See note, line 818.

1048 **Mercy** This was the supplication to a superior for a favour. It was much used in the formal language of 'courtly love' as the supplication of the lover to his 'goddess' for pity and favour.

1068 **nacioun** Used here in the sense of 'birth' (French 'naissance'), or 'upbringing' i.e. 'that anyone of my background . . .'

1081 **as an owle** The owl is a shy bird that keeps itself very much hidden in the day.

1084 **abedde ybroght** It was customary in the Middle Ages for the bride and bridegroom after the wedding party to be escorted to the bridal chamber with much enthusiasm by relatives and friends. This is a reference to the custom, for there was no joy or party in the wedding ceremony that had just taken place.

1090 **dangerous** Difficult, indifferent, off-hand. The word is not to be confused with the modern meaning. The word is frequently used in terms of 'courtly love', as it is here, with all the overtones of haughtiness, stiffness and arrogance. In other words, the very opposite to the '*courtesie*' and '*gentillesse*' expected of knights, particularly in their behaviour to women. See also note line 151.

1100 **Thou art so loothly** The theme of 'The Loathly Lady' or 'Transformed Hag' is found in many fourteenth century tales, both literary and popular. The story is the same – an ugly old hag, sometimes the victim of enchantment, and a handsome young knight. The choice offered the knight of having his bride beautiful in the day and ugly at night, or the other way round, is an old feature in the popular tales.

1109 **gentillesse** This was a very important word in medieval literature, and had many shades of meaning. The modern equivalent with the nearest meaning would be 'gentility', with all the understanding of rank and gentlemanly conduct. In Chaucer's time the meaning was more precise and was connected specifically with the background and behaviour of chivalry and knighthood – family and rank allied to good breeding and good manners.

1110 **old richesse** Literally, old riches or wealth, but with the meaning of 'with an ancient noble and wealthy family background'. Dante uses the same wording, '*antica ricchezza*'.

1117–18 This basis of the Christian argument was that our virtues are derived from Christ and not from our noble ancestors. This is the theme in Chaucer's Balade of Gentillesse.

1125–6 **wise poete of Florence** Dante Alighieri (1265–1321), born in Florence of a noble Florentine family. Dante, like Chaucer with English, established the Italian language as the literary language, displacing Latin. Dante is considered the greatest poet of Italy, and the Divine Comedy one of the landmarks in world literature. Inspired by his 'ideal lady', Beatrice, the poet describes his journey through Hell (Inferno) and Purgatory (Purgatorio), led by Virgil, and then up to Paradise (Paradiso) under the guidance of Beatrice.

1128–30 Dante in his 'Purgatorio' writes of the noble integrity (the 'probity' of man – 'probitate'; Chaucer's *Prowesse of man*') rising through the branches which represent the off-spring of a noble trunk or stock.

1139–45 A similar comparison is found in the work of Boethius, a learned poet of the sixth century and author of the philosophical work De Consolatione Philosophiae, one of the best known books in the Middle Ages. Chaucer translated the work under the tile of 'Boece'.

1140 **the mount of Kaukasous** The Caucasian mountains, a reference which is found in Chaucer's translation of Boethius to indicate a far-off land, so far-off that even the fame of Rome had not reached it.

1146–7 The point is made again that 'genterie', that mixture of good breeding and good manners, is not the 'natural' result of aristocratic birth and wealth.

1148 **doon hir operacioun** i.e. to carry out their natural functions.

1149 **in his kinde** i.e. according to its nature, i.e. the 'nature' of the person or thing determines the way it would behave.

1161 **strange** i.e. quite foreign to your person. 'Strange' in Middle English means 'foreign, external'. In the Portrait of the Wife of Bath in the *General Prologue* it mentions that she had many pilgrimages abroad: 'She hadde passed many a straunge strem' (line 464).

1165 **Valerius** One of the authors in Jankin's 'terrible book' from which the Wife tore out some pages (see lines 669–71). The work is attributed to Walter Map, a wit and cynic of the thirteenth century (see note, line 671). One can understand the Wife referring to this obscure writer, but it is difficult to expect such a name to be mentioned by an enchanted old hag.

1166 **Tullius Hostillius** A Roman ruler. From being a herdsman he rose to the highest rank, enjoying the highest honours and dignities.

1168 **Senek** Seneca, Roman writer, philosopher, dramatist and statesman who lived in the first century. Seneca was a great moralist and Rome's leading intellectual figure during the reign of the Emperor Nero.

Boece See note, lines 1139–45.

1182 **vicious** i.e. full of vice. Not our strong modern meaning.

1190 **knave** The meaning of 'knave' in the Middle Ages was still that of a page or servant, although there was a change in meaning to 'rogue' happening (compare line 253). We still use the original meaning when we describe the 'knave' of playing cards. The French equivalent of knave in the Middle Ages was *valet*, and this term was used for the equivalent of the 'knave' playing card, e.g. Knave of Spades was (and still is in modern France) called *Valet de Pique*.

1192 **Juvenal** Juvenal, the Roman Satirist of the first century. Considered to be the last great Roman satiric poet, and much admired as a thinker in the Middle Ages. His satires dealt mainly with life in Rome, attacking corruption and the follies of mankind. He was for a long time miserably poor and in one of his books of satires explains that he is leaving Rome where 'honest men cannot make a living and poverty entails scorn'.

1205 Because poverty, which was one of the main reasons given by the knight why he couldn't possibly marry the old hag, is a blessed state, according to the argument, then there can now be no reason for the knight's reluctance. The logic of the old hag is very similar to that used by the Wife in her Prologue, but the message is very different, except for the ultimate objective of 'maistrie'.

1208–9 **thogh noon auctoritee** The same statement is made by the Wife of Bath in the opening lines of her *Prologue*.

1236–7 This was, of course, the purpose of the story. The Wife told the story as an example (exemplum) of how things will always go well if, and only if, the husband is sensible enough to give all the control and authority to his wife.

1257–64 Chaucer often summarized, in a few lines, the conclusions of a tale. Here he sums up not only the 'lesson' of the tale, but the whole purpose in the life of the Wife of Bath.

Chaucer's art in *The Wife of Bath's Tale*
The character of the Wife of Bath

Alison is one of the most distinctive figures on the Canterbury pilgrimage. It would have been easy to pick her out, with her scarlet red hose (leggings) and hat as broad as a shield, riding among the rest of the company. Unlike the Prioress, the only other major female character described in the *General Prologue*, the Wife of Bath does not dress with much modesty or elegance. Her slightly flashy taste in clothes is matched by the physical details noted by Chaucer in the Tabard Inn: 'Boold was hir face and fair and reed of hewe.'

The account she gives of herself in her own *Prologue* shows that this boldness of appearance is paralleled by self-confidence in company and assertiveness in action. From the *General Prologue* we learn also that the Wife is proud of her social status – she is angry if any other woman goes to make an offering in church in front of her; that she is very well-travelled, having gone on pilgrimages in Europe and even three times to Jerusalem; that she is a little deaf, a fact of some significance in her life-story; and that she has been married five times and is therefore highly experienced in what Chaucer calls 'the olde daunce' of love.

Marriage is, of course, the Wife's business. She is – or expects to be – the managing director, while each husband in turn is permitted to be, at best, a shareholder. The business metaphor is apt because, at least in her first three marriages, Alison makes it clear that she sees marriage as a transaction. In exchange for herself, her body, she receives from these three 'goode men, and riche, and olde' the payment of 'hir (i.e. their) lond and hir tresoor'. There is no mention of money in her relationship with her fourth husband, but the notion of 'repayment' or revenge is evident in the Wife's account. Since this particular man was a 'revelour' and kept a mistress, the Wife ensures that she gets her own back:

'... I made folk swich cheere
That in his owene grece I made him frie
For angre, and for verray jalousie.'

She pays him back in his own coin, or, as she expresses it, 'I made him of the same wode a croce'.

The fifth husband, the clerk (scholar) Jankin, is distinguished from her other partners. He is the only one to be given a name. More importantly, she describes how she took him 'for love, and no richesse'. But the monetary considerations are still strong: she uses the lure of gold in his seduction (lines 575–84), hinting that she has more than just herself to offer him. When they are married, 'to him yaf I al the lond and fee/That evere me yeven therbifoore'. Ironically, the Wife gives up her riches for love – a reversal of the situation that existed in her first three marriages. But the Wife soon regrets her unguarded generosity and, when she finally outwits Jankin by a mixture of force and cunning, she once again takes control of her property and possessions. In one aspect, therefore, the Wife's conduct of marital affairs looks like economic warfare.

If money matters to Alison, then power is even more important. In keeping with the 'message' of the *Tale* – that women most desire to have the upper hand ('sovereynetee') – the Wife demonstrates how she puts her preaching into practice in her own life. Over her first three husbands, who are unceremoniously lumped together and treated as if they were one man, she maintains dominance by a policy of cunning and of verbal and physical aggression. This is in accordance with her doctrine that any husband must be 'bothe my dettour and my thral'. The men must labour in bed (215-6) and they must suffer her verbal assaults. She gives to her fellow-pilgrims an example of the lengthy battering in words (235–378) that she was accustomed to deliver to these unfortunate husbands. Through this tactic the Wife steals her husbands' ammunition by taking from them the abusive comments they might make about her and throwing such insults back at them with impudent contempt. This barrage of words was so intense and unremitting that the men were 'ful glade to excuse hem blive/Of thing of which they nevere agilte hir live.' All the time it was really the Wife who 'was in the gilt'. Attack is the best defence.

The Wife quite frankly admits that a desire for power was the governing principle of this part of her life:

'And thus of o thing I avaunte me,
Atte ende I hadde the bettre in ech degree,
By sleighte, or force, or by som maner thing . . .'

This need for supremacy operates with the fourth husband (whom the Wife so tormented that 'in erthe I was his purgatorie') and the fifth. After the uncharacteristic lapse, when the Wife is betrayed by love into surrendering everything to Jankin, she recovers her rightful position as head of the household and pays him back with interest: two blows to the one he gave her (the one that made her 'somdel deef') and his complete submission. He burns his anti-feminist book, symbol of his authority, and finally

'He yaf me al the bridel in myn hond,
To han the governance of hous and lond,
And of his tonge, and of his hond also.'

Notice how complete is the Wife's conception of control in these lines – control not merely over material possessions but over her husband's very words and actions.

Money and power; the use of sex to gain these objectives; the employment of cunning – even force if necessary – to keep her spouses in a state of subjection. We might assume from such a summary that the Wife of Bath is a thoroughly unlikeable character, fit to be bracketed with some of the more villainous figures on the pilgrimage. The response of most readers is different, however, and it is worth examining the process by which the Wife is rescued from the condemnation she might otherwise be expected to receive.

There is, first of all, her frankness. The fullness of Alison's revelations about herself, so that we are cast in the role of her 'gossip' (close friend, confidante) and get to know 'myn herte, and eek my privetee', is an initial step towards winning the listeners' confidence and sympathy. The only other character on the pilgrimage to offer such complete self-exposure is the Pardoner and, as with the Wife of Bath, we are entrusted with the ambiguous privilege of learning about the character's hidden motives and inner values which have been kept hidden – for reasons of self-protection – from the world at large.

Another important aspect of the Wife's character is that, although calculation and cunning have played a very large part in her relationships with men, she is herself by no means immune to the appetite for sex and love that she has exploited in others. This is particularly true of her last two marriages, in which affection and mutual enjoyment have a definite place and in which Alison's preoccupation with power and authority seems temporarily moderated. If marriage is viewed as a race – and this is one interpretation the Wife puts on it – then she is ahead of the first three husbands, level with the fourth and outdistanced for a while by the fifth. Of course, she puts on a final spurt and wins in the end!

She still speaks of Jankin, the fifth, affectionately despite his rough treatment of her.

'God lete his soule nevere come in helle!
And yet was he to me the mooste shrewe;
That feele I on my ribbes al by rewe,
And evere shal unto myn ending day.
But in oure bed he was so freesh and gay . . .'

Even after the crisis in their marriage, in which his authority was destroyed, they plainly had a very affectionate relationship:

'God helpe me so, I was to him as kinde
As any wyf from Denmark unto Inde,
And also trewe, and so was he to me.'

However grudging the Wife may have been in granting her favours to her first husbands (see lines 407–419), she was generous enough elsewhere. There is perhaps some inconsistency in the Wife's presentation of herself here: she indignantly denies that she provoked her fourth husband's jealousy by committing adultery ('Nat of my body, in no foul manere') but at other times she offers us a picture of herself as helplessly promiscuous. It is, she claims, her 'constellation', the position of the stars and planets at the time of her birth, that has made her what she is –

'That (i.e. her 'stars') made me I koude noght withdrawe
My chambre of Venus from a good felawe.'

In the same section of her prologue she depicts herself almost as a 'victim' of her appetite and the desire for affection:

'I ne loved nevere by no discrecioun,
But evere folwede myn appetit,
Al were he short, or long, or blak, or whit;
I took no kep, so that he liked me,
How poore he was, ne eek of what degree.'

(It should be noted that the phrase 'so that he liked me' is open to two interpretations: 'as long as he liked me' or 'as long as I found him attractive'. For the Wife affection and sexuality are closely linked.)

There is an element of self-deception in the Wife's attempt to transfer responsibility for her actions from herself to the 'stars'. It would obviously suit her to lay the 'blame' on some outside influence and, by so doing, to justify her behaviour. Nevertheless, astrology was a more respected subject in Chaucer's time than it is today, and although we cannot know how much credence Chaucer himself attached to it he was sufficiently interested to give astrological matters a prominent position in his poetry. The combination of Mars and Venus as influences over the wife can be traced in the make-up of her temperament. An astrological explanation of the wife's character might run as follows: Venus is a 'lucky' planet which bestows beauty and amorousness on her subjects, as well as a taste for music and dancing and (for female subjects) a love of fine clothes, perfumes and ornaments. Subjects of Venus marry more than once, and are usually happy in their marriages. The Wife of Bath has all these characteristics, but the 'gentleness of nature' which touches all true servants of Venus is missing. Mars was also in the sign of Taurus at the time of her birth. Now Mars was considered an evil and unlucky planet, with a red aspect and an aggressive and debasing influence. This was what coarsened the attributes the Wife had inherited from Venus, and added the hard determination and remarkable stamina that had worn down her husbands and caused them to surrender. This is the explanation the Wife gives in rather more concise terms:

'Venus me yaf my lust, my likerousnesse,
And Mars yaf me my sturdy hardinesse.'

We should not, of course, accept that this character is literally unable to be anything other than what she is. To believe that the Wife is somehow 'programmed' by forces outside her control is to diminish her and deprive her of the dignity of autonomous action. In any case Alison, even when presenting herself as the victim of her appetites or of the stars, is hardly regretful of the temperament she has been endowed with. Rather she rejoices in her vigour, her sexual urges, and her skilful employment of all the steps in love's 'olde daunce'.

The Wife, as should be apparent from what has been said, is presented – or presents herself – in a somewhat contradictory fashion. She speaks of the 'tribulation' which there is in married life but her enthusiasm for that state is still keen ('Welcome the sixte (husband), whan that evere he shal'). There is an ambivalence throughout the Wife's discussion of marriage. It may sometimes be a battlefield but it also provides a kind of shelter – particularly for women, we may suppose, in the Middle Ages. Alison hints at this when she tells us how she was never without 'purveiance/Of mariage' – to lack this 'foresight' would be to act like the mouse with only one hole to go to, she informs us with a proverbial flourish. She is a dominant woman, but one who is herself dominated by the desire for affection and sexual satisfaction. She endured her first husbands' lusts for the sake of 'wynning' (profit), yet at other times poverty or lack of rank means nothing to her provided 'that he (a would-be lover) liked me'. She is grudging and open-handed, devious and frank, capable of promiscuity and fidelity. These contradictions are not inconsistencies in Chaucer's characterization. They give living shape to a figure which cannot safely be left in one simple descriptive category.

The Wife of Bath does not apologize for her behaviour. She does not glorify her past nor does she sentimentalize it. One of her endearing features is her capacity to look back with a fine mixture of sadness and good spirits, as these well-known lines show:

'Unto this day it dooth myn herte boote
That I have had my world as in my time.
But age, allas, that al wole envenime,
Hath me biraft my beautee and my pith.
Lat go, farewel; the devel go therwith!
The flour is goon, ther is namoore to telle;
The bren, as I best kan, now moste I selle'

The final image, of selling the 'bran' now that the 'flour' is exhausted, is typical of the narrator and reminds us that a mercenary aggressiveness is never far from the Wife's mind. But there is also self-acceptance in the remark. She robustly faces up to the fact that the 'goods' she has on offer are not of the quality they once were. Her comments about age have a universal application but her nonchalance ('Lat go, farewel') is not to be found everywhere. If much of what she says elsewhere in the *Prologue* suggests a restless nature, the line, 'I have had my world as in my time', which is difficult to translate adequately, nevertheless hints at some fulfilment. Common sense, proverbial shrewdness, a slight coarseness and defiance are, characteristically, blended in the Wife's words in this excerpt.

A final aspect of Alison's character that should be noted is her sense of the theatrical. Look, for instance, at the way she combines speech and action in her outwitting of Jankin (797–810). It is an act. So too is the thundering monologue delivered against her first husbands, and the dream which she so cunningly recounts to the clerk (577–82), a fantasy in which 'al was fals'. She knows how to manipulate her audience and, if persuasion fails, how to bully it into submission. The Wife is as skilled as a politician at dealing with those who attempt to take her position at the centre of the stage, witness the practised way she deals with Pardoner and Friar. She is a tireless self-dramatizer. Her life, with all its conflict, humour, occasional bitterness and ultimate reconciliation provides her with the raw material for her 'act' and we are left in no doubt as to who is the principal player in her story.

Structure and argument in the *Wife of Bath's Prologue* and *Tale*

The Prologue

At first sight the *Prologue* appears unplanned, deriving whatever shape it may possess from the Wife's chronological account of her marriages. A closer examination, however, reveals the care with which Chaucer has established structure and order in this part of the poem. The Wife meanders and, at one point (585–6), loses her way altogether, but all the time she is following the route carefully laid down by her creator.

After a brief introduction *The Wife's Prologue* divides conveniently into two principal sections, which might be labelled 'theory' and 'practice'. The theoretical section (9–162) is made up of Alison's arguments in favour of marriage and remarriage; the practical section (193–828) is the narrative of herself and her five husbands. In between is the exchange between the Pardoner and the Wife (163–92) which serves to break up her monologue, to demonstrate her skill in dealing with anyone daring to interrupt her and, above all, to give the sense of a living response to what she is saying.

The two areas indicated above – 'life' and 'theory' – are not rigidly separated, but mingle with each other. During her learned defence of the married state the Wife makes frequent personal interjections – she wishes she could be 'refresshed' with half as many partners as King Solomon enjoyed; she has no intention of being 'daungerous' (stand-offish) in sexual relations – which somewhat undermine any pretensions to a cool, academic tone in her arguments. And during her lengthy autobiographical account she often refers to academic authorities, particularly those who have taken an anti-feminist position.

The Wife's knowledge of academic authors, which is of course really Chaucer's knowledge, is usually explained as having been gleaned from her fifth husband, Jankin the 'clerk of Oxenford'. This last partner was obviously a thoroughgoing anti-feminist, whose favourite pastime was to read aloud to his unwilling wife from a book stuffed with examples of female lechery and deceit. The material continued in this part of the *Prologue* (671–783) is drawn from French and Latin sources and is characteristic of medieval anti-feminist writing. Not surprisingly, the Wife reacts with exasperation to this sort of satire – it would be a different matter if women wrote the stories, she says.

This background gives a plausible enough explanation as to how Alison came to master such a broad field of learning hostile to herself and her sex. We may still feel, however, that a woman who sets such a premium on 'experience' (the first, emphatic word of the poem) gives too much space to a theoretical defence of her position and her behaviour. If she is so convinced of her rightness, and if she has enjoyed and profited from her life, why then does she need to treat her fellow-pilgrims to a weighty exposition of the relative merits of marriage, virginity etc?

One answer perhaps lies in her changing character: now that she has reached a more reflective middle-age she may wish to justify her past actions in the eyes of others – and in her own sight. A more probable explanation is that argument and debate are a means, not of arriving at the truth through persuasion and an exchange of views, but another method of establishing control over other people. It is as if the response which she was unable to give to the scholarly clerk during their marriage – for we are told that after he burned his book 'we hadden never debaat' – she is now giving to the pilgrims. In fact, she tends to assert rather than argue, and nobody is invited to disagree with her. Jumping from point to point, she tries to outwit the theological authorities at their own game. In other words, the Wife's personal philosophy, expressed with as much logic as she can muster, is another weapon in her formidable campaign to achieve 'sovereinetee' over the male enemy. With her usual fearlessness, even impudence, she seizes from the masculine stronghold its armoury of argument, learning, weighty allusion to Biblical and classical 'authorities', and turns the attack on all those who would deny women the right to live their lives as they please.

The topics covered by the Wife in this opening 'theoretical' section may be summarized as follows: remarriage (after the death of a partner) is not forbidden in the Bible, and no stipulation is made as to the number of husbands or wives one may have in succession. Marriage(s) would seem to be fully endorsed by God's instruction 'to wexe and multiplye', a text close to the Wife's heart, although it should be noted that she has not, in fact, produced any children. For support here she also refers to

Old Testament figures like Abraham and Jacob, who 'hadde wyves mo than two'. Virginity may be *commended* in the Bible (by St Paul) but it is not *commanded* for everyone – indeed how could it be? If everyone were chaste, then chastity itself would soon disappear, together with the human race! The Wife explains that different people can serve God in different ways, inside and outside marriage. Finally she appeals to common sense:

'Telle me also, to what conclusion
Were membres maad of generacion,
And of so parfit wys a wight ywroght?'

What the Wife argues for at the beginning of her speech may seem very remote to us. It is necessary, however, to remember the climate of opinion in which she was speaking (or Chaucer was writing). Interpreting Genesis literally, churchmen held woman, in the person of Eve, to be responsible for the fall of man and the expulsion from the Garden of Eden (see 715–9). A higher value was set on virginity than on marriage, at least on the latter in its sexual aspect. Remarriage might well be frowned on as improper, even immoral. All these beliefs are attacked, implicitly or explicitly, by the Wife and she uses the ammunition that her 'enemies' have already used against her, frequently citing the Bible in support of her viewpoint. However strained her arguments may sometimes look, we should remember the vulnerability of her position: it is impossible, she says at one moment, 'that any clerk wol speke good of wyves (here used in the general sense of 'women')'. For someone of the Wife's combative disposition, to be constantly attacked by authority is an invitation to take the battle into the enemy's own territory.

Beneath the surface of her reasoning we sense the real muscle and bone of her prejudices and preferences. She wishes to marry (frequently), and so she will discover arguments in favour of her doing so. She wants a husband not for any spiritual reason, but so that he 'shal be bothe my dettour and my thral'. The whole process of argument can be seen as an extension of her craving for control and revenge – the clerk had employed 'authority' as a weapon against the temporarily subdued Wife, so she now pays him (or at least his class) back in kind. As so often, speech here masquerades as something essentially reasonable but, in reality, has more to do with the speaker's inner emotional needs and urges.

The rest of the Prologue is given up to Alison's description of her differing relationships with her five husbands. Here there is some narrative variation, and a gentler and more humorous note is occasionally permitted. Along with the generalizations and proverbial observations concerning men and women are odd and revealing touches, as when she tells her fellow-travellers that she did not spend much on her fourth husband's tomb because it 'nis but wast to burye him preciously' or how, at the same man's funeral, she already had her eye on her next partner, Jankin:

'As help me God! whan that I saugh him go
After the beere, me thoughte he hadde a paire
Of legges and of feet so clene and faire
That al myn herte I yaf unto his hoold.'

Perhaps it is the openness, even innocence, of such 'confessions' that makes them, paradoxically, touching rather than tokens of heartlessness.

In the Wife's battle with her scholar-husband we see the final triumph of experience over bookish authority. It is victory in every aspect, physical, intellectual, psychological. The clerk is knocked into the fire, made to burn his book and finally abandons control of the household to Alison. We may feel that the Wife could consider her one blow, even if it did make her a little deaf, a price worth paying for this triumph. The *Prologue* can be interpreted, therefore, as a dramatized description of the antagonism between (female) experience and (male) authority, conceived both on a theoretical level and as an actual conflict in the real world. Love may finally conquer all, but it is a love imposed on the Wife's own terms; the *Prologue* is in itself proof of how different things would have been if, instead of men, 'wommen hadde written stories'.

The Wife of Bath's Tale

The *Tale* told by the Wife of Bath is usually viewed as the poor relation of the *Prologue*. It is inevitably overshadowed by the Wife's exuberant life-history, which is twice the length of what follows. Perhaps it would be more accurate to say that Alison's vital, sometimes bitter presence seems to be, in the *Tale*, subdued to the requirements of a narrative which lacks many of the qualities associated with the best of *The Canterbury Tales*. It is possible that Chaucer originally assigned another story to her and that she was given her present narrative in a later revision by the author. It is true that we hear the authentic tones of the Wife at one or two points in the *Tale* – when she has fun at the expense of friars (864–81), for example – but critical comment has often been directed at how different the tale is from its teller; how inappropriate, even incongruous, it is that the Wife should give over so large a portion of what she has to say to a lecture on the meaning of 'gentillesse' or the virtues of poverty.

The outline of the story of the Knight and the Loathly Lady, as it is sometimes called, was not of Chaucer's own invention. But it is his in its detail, development, pace and emphasis. It is easy to characterize the material in negative terms. It lacks real narrative urgency (unlike, say, *The Pardoner's Tale*); it is without any genuine interest in the complexities of individual human response (unlike stories told by other pilgrims such as the Knight, Merchant or Franklin); it does not possess the playfulness and ornamenation of a high-spirited piece such as *The Nun's Priest's Tale*.

Despite all this, we must not undervalue the *Tale*. It works effectively as narrative, as we are drawn forward firstly by our wish to know whether the knight will find the answer to the question posed by the ladies of King Arthur's court and secondly by our interest in the working-out of the bargain between him and the old woman. More importantly, the *Tale* reflects the preoccupations of its teller. Like the *Prologue* it can be divided into two sections. There is the life-and-death question which is satisfactorily resolved, but the solution to this, at about the half-way point in the story, ironically plunges the knight into another crisis and a misery which is almost as sharp. Rescued from the axe, he faces the prospect of a living death – as he sees it – with the ugly old woman.

After the lecture on his wedding-night, the knight is faced with a set of alternatives (see *Plot* p. 14 for details) but is unable to choose. He puts himself entirely in his wife's hands and, as a reward, she is transformed into a wife who is both beautiful and faithful. The parallels with the *Prologue* are apparent enough. Tranquillity comes to the household of the Wife and Jankin only when the latter has thrown away his book and his authority. Then, in recompense, she is 'as kinde/As any wyf from Denmark unto Inde,/And also trewe, and so was he to me.' Similarly the wife in the *Tale* promises to be 'good and trewe/As evere was wyf', after her new husband has surrendered his right to make decisions.

There is a larger parallel between *Prologue* and *Tale*. The first part of each deals with a subject – marriage and what women most want, respectively – on a 'theoretical' level. The second part handles the putting into practice of that theory: we see just how the Wife enthralled her husbands by a mixture of bullying and seductiveness; we learn how the fulfilment of what the *Tale* presents as women's strongest desire (for 'maistrie') makes for a harmonious marriage, satisfying to both husband and wife. In each piece, *Prologue* and *Tale*, there is a general movement from the level of ideas to the level of action.

The *Tale* shows us a man who is surrounded by, and at the mercy of, women. It is true that the story starts with an act of male brutality, the rape, but this is dealt with in a very perfunctory fashion by the Wife, suggesting that she does not regard it as being of much importance in itself, but is using it as a means of manoeuvring the knight into a position where he is subject to the dictates of various women. The queen sets the conditions by which he will save his life. After an unsuccessful quest the knight is returning home when he encounters the Loathly Lady who will provide him with an answer, provided that he performs 'the nexte thyng that I requere thee'. Doubly bound now, to the queen's court and to the old woman, he delivers his answer before a company of women – maids, wives, widows – with the queen herself 'sittynge as a justise'. Then the Loathly Lady demands her part of the bargain. The knight, as a man of honour (albeit somewhat stained), has no choice but to surrender to her. His role in the rest of the narrative is more or less confined to tossing and turning on his marriage-bed because his bride is 'so loathly and so oolde also'. His final act is to hand over to her the power of taking action. Only then, as has been noted, does he get his reward. The knight is almost entirely passive or ineffectual. Leaving aside the initial crime of rape, itself the antithesis of chivalrous behaviour, he does very little in the story. He fails in his quest (the old hag has to give him the answer) and by the end of the *Tale* he is too weary, after the long lecture from his new wife, to make even a show of independent thought or action. We might legitimately assume that there was something congenial to the Wife of Bath in her rather colourless portrait of an erring man who finds himself being handed round at the disposal of a company of females – it sounds like her kind of man.

It is plain that there is an element of wish-fulfilment in the *Tale*. In real life the Wife could promise fidelity and affection to a properly submissive husband, but even she could not roll back the years and counter the effects of age, which 'al wole envenyme'. In the fictional world of the *Tale*, the old wife can transform herself into the ideal of youth and beauty. The 'magical', loosely Arthurian setting allows this miracle of rejuvenation to occur. The Wife's robust common sense tells her that she must accept the fading of her attractions, but there is perhaps some small compensation in telling a story in which an old woman becomes a beautiful heroine.

Age is the last subject to be treated by the Loathly Lady in her lecture to the knight. As a result of his ungallant comments she offers him the ugly/faithful, beautiful/unfaithful puzzle. She also claims that the knight has reproached her for poverty. In fact he has not done this, but it is a familiar device in argument to attribute to one's opponent accusations or objections that have never actually been made and then, by overcoming them, to gain the illusion of victory and evade the real issue. The lengthiest piece of self-defence offered by the Loathly Lady – and the one that has provoked most critical comment – is her discussion of the meaning of 'gentillesse'. The knight has accused her of lacking breeding (she comes 'of so lough a kinde') but true 'gentillesse', she mainains, is the result of innate character rather than being born into the right family. 'Vertuous lyvyng' and 'gentil dedis' are the source of true worth and nobility, not the quality of our ancestors. The lines that Chaucer, or the Wife of Bath, gives to the newly wedded woman here, as well as the description of the blessings of poverty which follows, are examples of standard medieval moralizing. They are very conventional, but the subject of 'gentillesse' would have been of absorbing interest to Chaucer's audience, which would have been looking for a restatement of what they already believed rather than anything startlingly new.

To answer the question of why the Wife of Bath was concerned with the fairly rarefied subject of 'gentillesse' or the moral improvement offered by the state of poverty is not easy. One possible answer is that she, like the Loathly Lady, was once poor and low-born. If this cannot be said with certainty, it is safe to claim that she was not born to wealth or a good family. The whole history of her marriages indicates how hard Alison has struggled to establish herself materially and socially in the world. Her view of life is fundamentally competitive, not to say combative. She would therefore have some respect for a doctrine which proclaimed that to be 'gentil' was not the same as being well-born. Now a comfortable member of the middle-class, she would like to think that effort and character – not blood and ancestry – make one what one is. Poverty is obviously an unattractive state to her – why else would she have gone to such lengths to amass property and possessions from her first three husbands? – but we can speculate that she might have a desire to defend poverty, at least in theory, and to search for its 'virtues'. It is not a condition to which she would willingly return but she (in the person of the wife in the Tale) is prepared to defend it against the kind of aristocratic disdain of a 'chivalrous' knight who lumps together age, female ugliness and low breeding as things which repel him.

It has to be said, finally, that one can 'explain' why the Wife might be preoccupied with subjects such as 'gentillesse', but the measured tones in which her character discusses them is markedly different from the vigorous and individual note of the *Prologue*. The links between teller and Tale do often seem tenuous. Only at the end of her *Tale*, when Alison is speaking for herself rather than as a narrator of other people's actions, does she again sound like the familiar Wife of Bath, with her twinned appetites for sex and power:

'... and Jhesu Crist us sende
Housbondes meeke, yonge, and fressh abedde,
And grace t'overbide hem that we wedde...'

Whatever transformations may be brought about at the end of the *Tale*, some things do not change.

Grammar, pronunciation and versification

Chaucer's language, sometimes called Middle English, represents a transitional stage between Old English (or Anglo-Saxon) and what we speak today. By Chaucer's time English had become a blend of Saxon and the French brought across at the time of the Norman Conquest, but there were distinct dialects in different areas of the country (stronger than modern regional variations). Chaucer's own dialect was the East Midland and, largely because this was the variation of English used in court and government, it was this form of the language that became the standard one. Chaucer's English is recognizably close to us – perhaps closer than might at first sight appear – but there are differences in vocabulary and in the way words work. Such differences are no real barrier to understanding and enjoying Chaucer: the sense of the verse can usually be appreciated without precise grammatical knowledge and it can sometimes be helpful to pronounce aloud an unfamiliar-looking word, the meaning of which may be more apparent in its sound than in its spelling. The latter, incidentally, was not regularized in Chaucer's day, and the same word may be differently spelled in different parts of the text. Middle English was more strongly inflected than its modern counterpart, that is, there was greater variation in the endings of words. For example, where in modern English only the third person singular of the present tense is inflected ('makes', 'falls') in Middle English we find a number of variations to verb-endings in the present tense ('make, makest, maketh, maken).

Grammar

These very brief notes on grammar may be helpful:

Noun inflection is very similar to that used in modern English:

-es is almost invariably the mark of the possessive (genitive) case, e.g. 'mannes herte', 'preestes sone', and (e)s indicates the plural, e.g. 'hennes', 'bookes', 'humours'. There are a few exceptions to the standard possessive inflection, e.g. 'fader kin' means 'father's family'.

There are also irregular plurals, mostly familiar ones ('wommen', 'oxen'), a few not ('eyen').

Pronouns: it should be noted that there is no equivalent for 'its' in Middle English. 'His' is used for persons and things, e.g. 'the sonne in his ascencioun'. 'Hir' means both 'her' and 'their', but the context generally makes clear which is intended.

Sometimes the pronoun 'thou' is attached to the verb in a question, e.g. 'woldestow' meaning 'would you'.

The plural of 'that' is 'tho', not 'those'.

Verbs: changes between tenses are not dissimilar to those in modern English. Note that the past participle form of a verb is frequently indicated by the prefix y-, e.g. 'yseyled', 'ywarned'.

Adverbs: in modern English almost all adverbs end '-ly'. This was one of the endings used in Chaucer's day but we also find adverbs ending in '-e' and '-liche'.

Pronunciation

Words of English origin

Short vowels

'a' pronounced like 'a' in French *placer*; but not like 'a' in English 'cat'.

'e' pronounced like 'e' in Modern English 'men'.

'i' pronounced like 'i' in 'pin'. 'y' is often written for 'i', and has the same sound as 'i'.

'o' pronounced like 'o' in 'not'. Before letters written with a number of short strokes, like 'm, n,' and especially a combination of these two, 'o' is written for 'u', but should be pronounced like 'u', as for example, in 'comen, love, somer, monk'.

'u' pronounced like 'u' in 'pull', or like 'oo' in 'soot'; but not like 'u' in 'duke'.

Long vowels

It is often possible to recognize a long vowel by its being duplicated in writing. For example 'taak' contains a long 'a'; 'sooth' contains a long 'o'.

'a' pronounced like 'a' in 'father'.

'e' pronounced like 'e' acute or like 'e' grave in French. Only a knowledge of the origin of the words in Old English can guide the reader to distinguish between the close and open sounds, as they are called, in Chaucer; but the former sound is usually represented in Modern English by 'ee', and the latter by 'ea'. Modern English 'need' had a close vowel in Old English, where it was spelt 'nēd'; Modern English 'mead', a meadow, was 'mǣd' in Old English with an open vowel. As an indication that these two vowels had distinct sounds, we may note that Chaucer very rarely makes them rhyme.

'i' (often written 'y'), pronounced like 'ee' in 'feel'.

'o' pronounced either like 'o' in 'so', or like 'a' in 'call'. Chaucer recognizes the different pronunciations just as he distinguishes the two long 'e' sounds. In Modern English the former sound is represented by 'oo', as in 'soon' while the latter is like the vowel sound in 'note'.

'u' pronounced like 'oo' in 'soon'.

Diphthongs

'ai, ei, ay', and 'ey' (pronounced like the diphthong in 'day', though some authorities believe they were sounded like 'i' in 'line'.

'au, aw' pronounced like 'ou' in 'house'; but before the combination '-ght' like the 'o' in 'not'.

'eu, ew' pronounced like 'ew' in 'few'.

'oi, oy' pronounced like 'oy' in 'boy'.

'ou, ow' pronounced like 'u', or like 'au, aw'.

In words of French origin

Such of these words as had already become part and parcel of the everyday speech would obey the rules for the pronunciation of English vowel sounds; the others would retain the vowels of the French language, which were sounded much as they are today.

In unaccented syllables

The final '-e' so common at the end of a line and elsewhere is sounded like the second syllable of the word 'china'.

Consonants

The consonants had generally the same pronunciation as they have today, with certain slight modifications.

There were no silent consonants, unless, as some scholars believe, the 'g' before 'n' is not sounded.

'kn' is pronounced as in Modern German.

'gg' is pronounced like the 'dge' in Modern English 'ridge'.

'gh' as in modern German may be either palatal or guttural, according to whether it is preceded by a palatal or a guttural vowel.

'ng' is sounded as in southern English 'fin-ger', not as in 'sing-er'.

'th' (initial) is sounded as in 'thin', not as in 'then'.

'ch' in words of both English and French origin is pronounced like the 'ch' of Modern English 'choose'.

'w' before 'r' is pronounced like a rapidly sounded 'oo'.

'h' in words of French origin and in words like 'he, him', which are rarely emphasized, is silent; but in most words of English origin an initial 'h' is sounded. Where the metre demands that a final '-e' should be elided before an 'h', that 'h' is silent.

Final 'f' is sounded as 'f', and not as 'v'.

Final 's' is sounded as 's', and not as 'z'.

Chaucer's use of the final -e

It is important to say something about the function of the final -e found at the end of many words in Chaucer's verse. At the beginning of the fourteenth century these were generally sounded as separate syllables, but by the end of the century they were coming into disuse. In Chaucer's verse the final -e may represent an inflexional change in a noun, an adjective, or a verb; or it may be what is left of a word-ending in Old English. There are many explanations of this termination, and the following rules usually apply in Chaucer.

1 The final -e is usually sounded, except when
(a) it is slurred over before a word beginning with a vowel (e.g. Of deerne love he koudeand of solas): before certain words beginning with 'h'; any part of the verb to have (e.g. a clerkhadde litherly biset his while); the adverbs heer, how, and a silent 'h' as in honour, him and hem (e.g. For for no cry hir maide koudehim calle).
(b) it is sometimes dropped in some words in common use as were, wolde.

2 The final -e should always be sounded at the end of a line.

Versification

Chaucer's verse is not difficult to read. As Professor Manly remarks 'the general principles of stress and movement in Chaucer's language and in his verse-patterns are, so far as we can discover, essentially the same as for present English'. The main difference is that a great many of Chaucer's words end in an unstressed final *-e, en,* or *-es.* It has already been mentioned that the final *-e* of any Chaucerian line must always be pronounced (as the final *-a* is pronounced in China), together with other final syllables within the line itself if the verse is to scan. Chaucer was, however, a master craftsman, with an ear for subtle rhythm, and in practice many final syllables were either slurred or suppressed altogether.

The Wife of Bath's Prologue and Tale is written in what are called heroic or decasyllabic couplets. Each line has ten syllables, normally, and the lines rhyme in pairs. The ten syllables in a line are divided into five groups of two syllables, known as feet. In most lines an unaccented syllable begins the foot, followed by an accented one. Such a line is 36:

'İ trówe hė háddé wivės mó thȧn oón.'

However, a long poem written entirely in such a metre would become monotonous, and it was for hearers and not readers that

Chaucer addressed himself. (In Corpus Christi College, Cambridge, there is a manuscript of Chaucer's *Troilus and Criseyde*, the frontispiece of which shows the poet reading to the court of Richard II.) A common method for preventing the monotony of a long series of decasyllabic lines (in classical terminology, the iambic pentameter) is to add an extra syllable at the end of a line, a practice found in Shakespeare's later plays. Chaucer adopts this practice by ending with a word in which the final syllable ends in an unstressed *-e*. An example of this found in lines 125 and 126:

'Şò thát thė clérkės bé nȧt wiťh mė wróthė.'
'I séy tħis, thát thėy mákėd bén fòr bóthė.'

Each line of the couplet has eleven syllables, the last being an unstressed *-e*. Often the final syllable is *-es*, as in lines 13 and 14.

Another variant is seen in line 60, where there are nine syllables only, the unstressed syllable of the first foot being omitted:

Thát hẏe Gód dėfendėd máriáge.

So, by varying the number of syllables in a line, Chaucer adds greater freedom and variety of movement to his verse. There is also another method for varying the rhythm of a line. In each decasyllabic line there is a pause known as a 'caesura'. Usually it is found near the middle of the line, that is after the fourth or fifth syllable; but Chaucer realized that the monotony which a regular position of the pause would give to a line could be overcome by varying the positioning of the caesura. We find that while the first line, 'Experience,/though noon auctoritee' has the pause after the fourth syllable, there are many cases of lines where the pause is placed sometimes nearer the beginning and sometimes nearer the end. Lines 6 and 11 are cases in point.

All these departures from a rigid standard have the effect of introducing variety into the verse, bringing with it gracefulness and easy rhythm which did not characterize the works of Chaucer's contemporaries, particularly those like Langland who wrote in the Old English verse-form of an elaborate alliterative structure where one of the stresses in the first half of the line must begin with the same letter as the first stress of the second half.

The opening lines from the Prologue of *Piers Plowman*, an almost exact contemporary of *The Canterbury Tales*, illustrate how far Chaucer's versification had developed.

In a somer sesoun. whan soft was the sonne,
I shope me in shroudes. as I a shepe were
In habite as an heremite. unholy of workes,
Went wyde in this world. wondres to here.

Compare these lines with the opening lines of the *Prologue* to *The Canterbury Tales*, and it is easy to understand why Chaucer's poetry has been referred to as 'the liquid music of language'.

Whan that Aprille with his shoures soote
The droghte of March hath perced to the roote
And bathed every veyne in swich licour
Of which vertu engendred is the flour.

General questions

1 Discuss the struggle between 'experience' and 'authority' in the *Prologue*.

Guideline notes

'Experience' is the first and emphasized word in *Prologue*. Wife does not need to be supported by 'auctoritee' to speake 'of wo that is in mariage' – her own life, and no theory, is behind everything she says. 'Authority' in Middle Ages was masculine prerogative and could convey double meaning: it has the sense of right, power of command (which husband might be expected to have over wife), and also the sense of 'authoritative statement' (drawn from Bible etc.) which would be brought forward in argument. Men like Jankin would have knowledge and learning to use such authorities – women, on the whole, would not; the Wife complains that men not only use such texts against women but that they are the only ones who have had chance to write. Men therefore have twofold 'authority' – they obtain backing from scriptural sources and anti-feminist texts to reinforce social and economic power they already possess over opposite sex. Wife will not tolerate this situation. She has been born with her weapons, rather than acquiring them 'unfairly' like men. She generalizes:

'Deceite, weping, spinning God hath yive
To wommen kindely (i.e. naturally), whil that they may live.'

Elsewhere she claims, 'I folwed ay my dames loore' – her learning comes, not from books, but either from her mother or from native wit (both interpretations fit the line). Her version of 'authority' is subversive, designed to deceive and outwit men. She learns, too, from experience (with five husbands and probably other lovers besides) and employs common sense (often seen as opposite of bookish or intellectual learning). All this so that she can gain 'authority' in other sense of power, control over men. Note final irony that she too uses 'masculine-style' logic, Biblical reference etc. to 'prove' her case on marriage. Conflict seen most clearly in marriage to clerk, who finally submits to Wife and loses all claim to authority of either sort.

2 The Wife of Bath is considered to be the most vivid and complex of Chaucer's character studies. In what way does Chaucer illustrate her character?

3 'The need for power is a stronger urge for the Wife than that for sex or love.' Do you agree?

4 Summarize the argument about marriage in *The Wife of Bath's Prologue*.

5 What sort of character has the Wife of Bath? Would you like her as a person? Illustrate.

6 Chaucer is a master of comic poetry. Discuss this with reference to the *Prologue*.

7 Discuss the importance of the *Prologue* to the plot of the *Tale*.

8 'Implicit in everything the Wife says is the belief that the natural relationship between men and women is one of hostility, if not open war.' How far do you consider this an accurate statement?

9 Does the Wife of Bath's character shown in her *Prologue* match the portrait of her sketched in the *General prologue*?

10 Discuss the Wife of Bath's tactics in gaining supremacy over her husbands.

11 'Chaucer is a supreme artist of story-telling' – how far is this borne out by *The Wife of Bath's Tale?*

12 Chaucer uses a variety of proverbs or common folk-expressions. Quote a few and explain their meanings.

13 What use does Chaucer make of the 'Arthurian' setting to the *Tale*?

14 What do we learn from the whole poem about life in Chaucer's time?

15 What differences do you see between the tone and atmosphere of the *Prologue* and the *Tale* told by the Wife?

16 Discuss the structure of the plot of the *Tale*.

17 Summarize the arguments about 'gentillesse' and poverty in the *Tale* and consider their significance for the Wife.

18 As an additional pilgrim on the way to Canterbury, write a letter (not in Middle English) to a friend describing your reaction to the Wife's presence and her words.

19 'In the end, reconciliation between the sexes is more important to the Wife than the victory of one side or the other.' How far do you consider this statement to be true?

20 Why should we still read *The Wife of Bath's Prologue and Tale?*

Further reading

The Canterbury Tales, translated by Nevil Coghill (Penguin, 1951)

For Chaucer's life and material on *The Canterbury Tales* as a whole see:

Geoffrey Chaucer of England, Marchette Chute (reissued 1977)

The Life and Times of Chaucer, John Gardner (Jonathan Cape, 1977)

An Introduction to Chaucer, Hussey, Spearing and Winny (CUP, 1965)

Chaucer's World, ed. M. Hussey (CUP)

On *The Wife of Bath's Prologue and Tale* see:

The Poet Chaucer, Neville Coghill (1967)

The Canterbury Tales, D. Pearsall (1985) (for an extended essay on *The Wife of Bath*)

The Canterbury Tales: A Casebook ed. J. J. Anderson (1974) (for the essay 'Irony in the Wife of Bath's Tale' by Tony Slade)

Glossary

abedde *to bed.*
abide *abide, wait, remain.*
abroche *broach, open up.*
a-caterwauled *a-caterwauling.*
accordinge *agreeing.*
acorded *agreed, reconciled.*
adoun *down.*
again *against (in answer to,* l.675*) (in front of before,* l.1000*).*
agast *aghast, horrified.*
agilte *guilty of.*
agoon *ago.*
agrief *ill, amiss.*
al *although, all.*
al and som *everyone, everything, the sum total.*
alenge *wretched, miserable.*
algate(s) *always, in every way.*
allies *relatives.*
allone *alone.*
al so *just as.*
always, alwey *always.*
amended *corrected, put right, improved.*
amendere *improve.*
a-morwe *tomorrow, next day.*
angre *anger.*
a-night *at night.*
annexed *attached, joined to.*
anon *at once, forthwith.*
answeren *answer.*
apert *openly, in public.*
apparaille *apparel, dress.*
appetit *appetite.*
a-rewe *in a row.*
array *dress, attire, furnishing, arrangement, order, method* (l.235).
arriven *arrive at, come to.*
artow *are you (art thou).*
ascendent *ascendant in astrology, the degree of the eliptic that is rising at a given time* (see note l.609 et seq.).
assailled *assailed, attacked.*
assay *test, trial.*
assayed *tested, tried out.*
asterte *escape, burst out.*
astrologien *astrologer.*
atte *at me.*
attendance *attentiveness, service.*
auctoritee *authority.*
auctour *author.*
audience *assembly, hearing (in open assembly,* l.1032*).*
auncestre *ancestor.*
avante, avaunte *vaunt, boast.*
aventure *chance, luck, by accident.*
Averill *April.*
aviseth *considers, deliberates.*
a-werke *to work.*
axe *ask.*
ay *always.*

ba *kiss.*
bacin *basin.*
bad *bade, commanded.*
backward *backwards.*
bar, baar *bore, possessed.*
bareyne *barren.*
barly-breed *barley bread.*
be war *be wary, take care.*
been (ben) *be, are.*
beere *bier.*
benedicite *bless ye (the Lord).*
ber *bear.*
berd *beard.*
bere *bear (oneself), behave.*
bere on honde *deceive, mislead.*
bernes *barns.*
best *beast, animal.*
bet, bettre *better.*
bete *beaten.*

bicam *became, suited.*
bifel *befell, happened.*
biforn *before, in front.*
bigon *provided, established.*
bigonne *began.*
biheste *promise.*
bileere *believe.*
bigquethe *bequeath.*
biraft(e) *bereft, deprived of.*
biseke *beseech, implore.*
bishrewe *curse.*
bisie *busy.*
bisinesse *busyness, diligence, care.*
bistowe *bestow, spend.*
bithinke *think, imagine.*
bitokeneth *betokens, signifies.*
bitore *bittern.*
bitterly *painfully, sharply.*
bitwixt *between.*
biwreyed *betrayed, revealed.*
blisful *blissful, happy.*
blisse *bliss, happiness.*
blissed *blessed.*
blive *quickly, forthwith.*
bobance *boast, presumption.*
bode *bade, commanded.*
boghte *bought.*
bombleth *booms.*
bon *bone.*
bonde *bound.*
booste *boast.*
boote *good, benefit.*
bord *board, table.*
borel *coarse woollen clothes.*
beren *born.*
born, borne *borne.*
bounden *bound.*
bountee *goodness, virtue, excellence.*
bour *bower, bed-chamber.*
bowen *bow down, give way.*
breed *bread.*
bren *bran.*
brenne *burn.*
brenneth *burns.*
brent *burnt.*
breste *burst, break.*
breyde *started, woke up.*
bridel *bridle, control.*
brinne *burn.*
burghes *boroughs, towns.*
but (if) *unless, except, if.*
by *with respect to, concerning.*
bye *buy (bring on,* l.167*).*

cacche *catch, take.*
calle *hair-net, head-dress.*
cam *came.*
care *care, anxiety.*
cas *case (subject, matter,* l.165*); (in any respect,* l.665*).*
cast *cast, throw.*
certeinly *certainly, for sure.*
certes/certeyn *assuredly.*
chaast *chaste.*
chaffare *wares, merchandise.*
chalenge *challenge, claim.*
chamberere *chambermaid, lady's maid.*
chambre *(bed)room.*
charge *load burden, responsibility.*
charitee *charity, charitable works.*
cheep *(market), market-price, bargain.*
cheere *appearance, behaviour.*
chees *choose.*
chepe *trade, bargain.*
cherl *churl, low-born fellow.*
chese *choose.*
cheste *chest, box, trunk; coffin.*
chidde *chided, scolded, reproached.*
chide *chide.*
chiertee *fondness, affection.*
chiste *see 'cheste'.*
clamour *clamour, outcry.*
clawe *rub, scratch.*
clene *clean, pure, fresh.*
clepe *call.*
cleped *called.*
clerk *'cleric', student, scholar.*
clooth *cloth, garment, covering.*
clothes *clothes, material.*
cokewold *cuckold.*
colour *colour, appearance; excuse, pretence.*

comanden *command, direct.*
compaignye *company.*
comth *comes.*
conclusion *intention, purpose.*
conseil *counsel, secret.*
conseille *advise, counsel, recommend.*
conseilling *advising.*
constellacioun *constellation, combination of heavenly bodies or influences.*
constreyned *constrained, compelled.*
continueel *continual.*
contraried *opposed.*
contrarious *contrary, perverse.*
contrarius *contrary, different.*
coost *coast, country, land.*
corps *corpse.*
costage *cost, expense.*
coveiteth *covets, desires.*
coverchief *head-scarf, head-dress.*
cow *chough.*
crave *crave (for), beg.*
crispe *crisp, curly.*
Crist *Christ.*
Cristen *Christian.*
croce *cross.*
cure *care, heed, attention.*
curius *carefully or skilfully made.*
curtin *curtain.*
custume *custom, habit.*

daliaunce *chat, gossip; dalliance, flirtation.*
dampnacioun *damnation.*
dampned *condemned, damned.*
dart *dart, spear.*
daun *Dan, Master (Mr).*
daunce *dance.*
daunger *disdain, indifference.*
daungerous *indifferent, difficult, disdainful, grudging.*
daunted *intimidated, terrified.*
dawed *dawned.*
debaat *debate, argument.*
dede *deed, act.*
dedis *deeds, acts.*
deed *dead.*
deef *deaf.*
deel *part, bit.*
deere *dear, expensive.*
defended *forbade.*
degree *degree, rank, status.*
delit *delight, pleasure.*
derkeste *darkest.*
desiren *desire.*
desolat *dejected.*
despit *spite, anger.*
despitus *spiteful, cruel.*
desport *sport, amusement, diversion.*
dettour *debtor.*
devise *devise, contrive, imagine.*
devine *guess, declare.*
devocioun *devotion.*
deyde *died.*
deye *die.*
deyntee *estimation, value, worth; delight, pleasure.*
dide *did.*
diffinicioun *restriction, imitation.*
dighte *do, have an affair, be with.*
diligence *diligence, heedfulness.*
discrecioun *discretion, prudence.*
disfigure *disfigurement, deformity.*
dishonour *disgrace, shame.*
disparaged *disgraced, dishonoured.*
dispence *expenditure, extravagance.*
displeseth *displeases, offends.*
disport *sport, amusement, pleasure.*
disposicioun *disposition, nature.*
diverse *diverse, different.*
doon *do, done.*
dorste *dared.*
dostow *do you (dost thou).*
dotage *dotage, senility.*
dotard *imbecile, fool.*
doute *doubt.*
doutelees *doubtless.*
draughte *draught.*
drede *doubt, question.*
dronke(n) *drunk.*

dronkenesse *drunkenness.*
dropping *dripping, leaking.*
drow *drew, approached.*
due *duke.*
dwelle *dwell, remain, stay.*
dyde *would die.*

ech a side *on every side.*
eek *also.*
eelde *old age.*
eftsoones *immediately after.*
elde *old age.*
eldres *elders, ancestors.*
elles *else.*
emperice *empress.*
empoisoned *poisoned.*
enchanted *bewitched.*
enforce *strengthen.*
engendreth *creates, produces.*
engendrure *procreation.*
enquere *enquire, question.*
ensample *example.*
entendeth *intended, aims.*
entente *intuition.*
entremette *interrupt, interfere.*
enverime *poison, corrupt.*
envie *envy.*
er *before.*
ere *ear.*
erl *Earl.*
erthe *earth.*
ese *entertainment, pleasure.*
esed *pleased, satisfied.*
est *east.*
estaat *social rank, position.*
eterne on live *immortal.*
even *evening.*
everemo *all the time, constantly.*
everich *everyone.*
every deel *every part, every bit.*
exaltacioun *(astrological). The position in which a planet exerts its strongest influence.*
exaltat *exaltat, in great influence and power.*
excepcioun *objection.*
expres *expressly, clearly, explicitly.*
eyleth *ails.*

fader *father.*
fadres *father's.*
faierye *fairies, fairy-folk.*
faille *fail.*
fair *attractive, pleasant.*
faire *kindly, agreeably, well.*
fairnesse *attractiveness, good looks.*
fals *false.*
falsy *falsely, treacherously.*
falwes *fallows, fallow ground.*
fantasie *fancy, desire, inclination; whim.*
fare *fare, go; behave.*
fareth *behave.*
fast(e) *closely, tight, secure* (l.283), *near, close by* (l.970), *hard, eagerly* (l.672).
fawe *glad, willing, fond.*
fee *possessions, property.*
feeldes *fields, meadows.*
feelinge *emotional character.*
feend *fiend, devil.*
feeste *feast.*
felawe *fellow, chap.*
fer (forth) *far.*
fere *fear.*
ferthe *fourth.*
fest *fist.*
fet *fetched, carried.*
fey *faith.*
feyred *feigned, pretended, dissimulated.*
fil(le) *fell.*
filthe *filth, shame.*
fine *finish, end.*
firy *fiery.*
fit *exciting situation or experience, mood, feeling.*
fle *flee, run away.*
fo *foe, enemy.*
folwed *followed.*
fonde *try, endeavour.*
foore *path, footsteps.*
forbede(th) *forbid(s).*
forbere *forbear, endure.*

forgat *forgot.*
forgo *forgo, give up, lose.*
fors *force, importance, consequence.*
forthermo *furthermore, moreover.*
foryene *forgive.*
foul(e) *foul, vile, ugly, wretched, bad, disgraceful* (l.485).
fouler *uglier.*
freendes *friends.*
freletee *frailty, weakness of the flesh.*
frely *freely, generously.*
frere *friar.*
frete *eat, devour, consume.*
frie *fry.*
fro *from.*
ful *very.*
fulfild *filled.*
fulfille *fulfil, satisfy.*
fully *fully, completely.*
fyn *fine, pure.*

gale *sing, cry out, exclaim.*
galle *sore spot.*
galwes *gallons.*
game *game, festival, party.*
gan *did.*
gat-tothed *gap-toothed.*
gay *merry, lively, well-dressed.*
geestes *tales, stories.*
generacioun *reproduction.*
generally *in general, as a general rule.*
genterie *gentry, nobility.*
gentil *of gentle birth and charcter, noble.*
gentillesse *gentlemanly conduct, good breeding and manners.*
gentils *gentlemen.*
gentrie *of gentle birth.*
gesse *guess, suppose.*
gete(n) *got, obtained.*
gilt *guilt, sin.*
giltelees *guiltless, innocent.*
gites *gowns, dresses.*
glad(e) *glad, happy.*
gladly *gladly, happily, eagerly.*
glose *interpret, explain* (l.119), *flatter, cajole* (l.509).
glosen *comment upon.*
good *goods, possessions, wealth* (l.310), *benefit, advantage* (l.231).
goost vb *goes;* sb *ghost, spirit* (l.986).
gossib *gossip, friend, relation.*
governance *government, control.*
grace *grace, favour; fortune* (l.746); *mercy, favour,* (l.895).
grave *buried.*
grece *grease.*
greet *great.*
green *greensward, grass.*
greve *grieve, upset.*
grint *grinds.*
grisly *terrible, horrible.*
grucche *grumble, murmur.*
grucching *grumbling.*

habitacioun *habitation, dwelling.*
hadden *had.*
half *behalf.*
halles *halls.*
halt *holds.*
halwes *shrines.*
han *have.*
happed *happened, chanced.*
hardinesse *physical vigour, stamina, healthiness, lustiness.*
harneys *harness, equipment.*
hastow *have you (hast thou).*
haukes *hawks.*
hawe *haw, hawthorn berry.*
heed *head.*
heer *hair.*
heere *hear, listen to.*
heeste *behest, order.*
heigh *high, noble.*
helde *hold.*
hele *conceal.*
helpeth *helps.*
hem *them(selves).*
hende *polite, courteous, well-mannered.*
hente *seized.*
herbes *herbs.*

heres *hair.*
heritage *heritage, inheritance.*
herkre(th) *listen.*
herte *heart.*
hevynesse *heaviness, sadness, dejection.*
hidestow *do you hide (hidest thou).*
hight *promised.*
highte *was called.*
him *himself.*
hir *their.*
hire *her* (l.533); *hire, reward, payment* (l.1008).
holde *hold, keep; held to, obliged* (l.135); *deem, account* (l.523).
holden *thought of, considered.*
holour *lecher, adulterer.*
hond *hand.*
honour *honour, respect, good reputation.*
hool *whole.*
hoolly *wholly.*
hooly *holy.*
hoom *home.*
hoot *hot.*
hors *horses.*
hoten *be called, named.*
hou *how.*
housbondrie *husbandry, household goods.*
hye *high.*
hyeste *highest, best.*

ilke *same.*
impossible *impossibility.*
in *inn, dwelling.*
in honde *in hand, in control of.*
inclinacioun *influence.*
incubus *evil spirit.*
Inde *the Indes.*
in-feere *together.*
iren *iron, axe* (l.906).
ivel *wit.*
ivel preef *bad luck to you.*

jalousie *jealousy.*
jangleresse *chatterbox.*
jape *trick, joke.*
jolitee *jollity, merriment, sport.*
joly *jolly, merry, lively.*
jolynesse *cheerfulness, amusement.*
juggement *judgement, discretion.*
justice *judge.*

kan *know (how), understand.*
kaynard *dotard, old fool.*
keep *care, heed.*
kep *regard, watch, vigilance.*
kepe *keep, preserve, take care of.*
kept *preserved.*
kichenes *kitchens.*
kike *kick.*
kinde *nature, race, stock, natural disposition.*
kindely *natural, by nature.*
kitte *cut.*
knave *servant, page; servant, rogue* (l.253).
knowen *discover, learn.*
koude *could, knew how to.*

lasse *less.*
large (at) *at large, free* (l.322).
lat(be) *let be.*
latter *later.*
lavour *wash basin.*
lawe *custom, fashion.*
lecchour *lecher.*
leef *leaf, page.*
leere *learn.*
leeste(atte) *at the least.*
leeve *dear.*
legendes *life stories, biographies.*
lemman *lover.*
lenger *longer.*
leon *lion.*
leonesse *lioness.*
lest *please, wish.*
lete *let, allowed; leave, forsake* (l.31).
lette *be hindered.*
lettest *hinder.*
leve vb. *give leave, permit;* sb. *leave, permission* (l.908).

leveful *permissible.*
levene *lightning flash.*
levere *rather.*
leyser *leisure.*
licence *licence, permission.*
lie *blaze.*
lief *dear, beloved.*
lige *liege.*
lightly *easily, quickly.*
liked *attracted.*
likerous *lecherous.*
likerousnesse *lecherousness.*
liketh *pleases.*
liking *pleasure, enjoyment.*
likne *liken, compare.*
limitacioun *limit, allocated district.*
limitour *limiter, friar with an allocated district.*
linage *lineage.*
line *line, family descent.*
list(e) *pleasure, wish, desire, ear* (l.634).
litel *little, small.*
lith *lies.*
live *life.*
lives *biographies.*
loke *lock.*
lond *land.*
loore *lore, teaching.*
loothly *loathsome, repulsive.*
lordinges *lords, gentlemen.*
lorel *wretch.*
lough *laughed (*l.672*)*, adj. *low.*
love *lover.*
lowe *low, wretched.*
lust vb. *pleases (*l.416*)*, sb. *lust, pleasure, delight.*
lusty *lusty, vigorous.*
lyen *lie.*

made *made, composed, wrote.*
maden *made, caused.*
magestee *majesty.*
maide *maid, virgin.*
maidenhed *maidenhead, virginity.*
maister *master, lord.*
maistow *may you (mayest thou).*
maistrie *mastery, superiority.*
make *mate.*
malencolie *melancholy, sullenness.*
maner(e) *kind, manner, fashion.*
manly *manly, clear and loud, confidently.*
many on *many a one.*
Marcien *subject of (influenced by) Mars.*
mareys *marsh.*
martes *of Mars.*
mate(e)re *matter, affair, subject, business.*
matins *matins, morning prayers.*
maugree *in spite of.*
me *myself.*
mede *meadow.*
meene *mean.*
mekely *meek.*
mencion *mention, statement.*
meschance *misfortune.*
meschief *mishap, injury.*
mette *dreamed.*
might *might, power, ability.*
mighte *could.*
mire *mire, mud.*
mirie *merry, happy, gay.*
mirily *happily, merrily.*
mirthe *joke.*
misavise *misbehave.*
mite *insect.*
mo *more.*
mooder *mother.*
mooste *most, greatest.*
moot *may, must.*
mooten *must.*
mordred *murdered.*
morne *mourn.*
morwe *morning.*
morweninges *mornings.*
most(e) *must.*
motthes *moths.*
muchel *much.*
murmur *grumbling.*
myn *mine, my.*

nacioun *birth, background,*

upbringing.
nam *am not.*
namely *particularly.*
namo *no other.*
namoore *no more.*
nath *has not.*
natheless *none the less, nevertheless.*
natureel *natural.*
natureelly *naturally, by nature.*
ne *not, nor.*
nece *niece.*
necligence *negligence, neglect.*
nedely *of necessity.*
nekke-boon *neck bone, neck.*
nel *will not.*
nice *foolish, ignorant.*
nicetee *nice little thing, fancy, treat.*
nigard *niggard, miser.*
nil *will not.*
nis *is not.*
niste *knew not.*
noblesse *nobility, high rank.*
noghte *not, not at all.*
nolde *would not, do not wish.*
nombre *number, quantity.*
nones (for the) *nonce, for the time or occasion.*
noon *no, none.*
norice *nurse.*
ny *near.*

octogamie *octogamy, marrying eight times.*
of *off.*
office *employment, practical use.*
ones (onis) *once.*
oon *one.*
oore *ore.*
oother *other (person).*
open-heveded *bare-headed.*
operacioun *operation, action, performance.*
opinion *opinion, belief.*
oppressioun *violation.*
oratories *chapels or closets for private devotion.*
ouch *necklace, clasp.*
out of doute *without a doubt.*
oute *set out, exhibit, show.*
outher *either.*
outrely *utterly, absolutely.*
over al *everywhere.*
over bide *outlast.*
owene *own.*

pace *pass, leave.*
pacient *patient, resigned.*
paid *satisfied.*
parage *birth, rank, lineage.*
paramour *lover, mistress.*
paraventure *perhaps.*
pardee *goodness, by God.*
parfit *perfect.*
pees *peace.*
perree *jewellery, precious stones.*
persevere *endure, continue.*
persone *person.*
pestilence *pestilence, plague.*
peyne *pain, grief, distress; trouble, care.*
peyntede *painted.*
pie *magpie.*
pine *agony, torment, suffering.*
pistel *(epistle) message, information.*
pith *vigour.*
pitously *piteously.*
plante *plant, cutting (piece of wood).*
plesance *pleasure.*
pleye *play, entertain or amuse oneself.*
pleyes of miracles *miracle plays.*
pleyne *complain.*
plight vb. *plucked, pulled out* (l.790), sb. *pledge* (l.1009).
poure *pour over, gaze at.*
poverte *poverty.*
povre *poor.*
praktike *practical experience.*
preamble *preamble, prologue, introduction.*
preambulacioun *preambling, introduction.*
precept *direction, instruction.*

preche *preach, lecture.*
prechestow *do you preach?*
preching *preaching.*
prechour *preacher.*
precious *precious, valuable.*
precius *fastidious, over-nice, particular.*
preciously *expensively.*
prees *press, crowd.*
preesse *press (on, forward).*
preest *parish priest.*
preferre *is preferred to, takes precedence over.*
prente *print, mark.*
preye preyeden *prayed, begged.*
preyse *praise.*
preysed *praised.*
priketh *pricks, spurs.*
pris *price, value, worth, excellence.*
privee *(in) private.*
prively *privately, secretly.*
privetee *private affairs.*
propre *one's own.*
proprely *properly, appropriately, exactly.*
prowesse *prowess, excellence, probity.*
prys *price, value, worth, excellence.*
pured *pure, refined.*
purgacioun *purgation, purging of bowels.*
purgatorie *purgatory, hell.*
purpos *purpose, intention.*
pursute *pursuit, petition.*
purveiance *foresight, forethought.*
purveye(d) *provide(d).*

queynte sb. *female organ;* adj. *quaint, curious, peculiar.*
quite *requite, repay.*
quitte *requited, repaid.*
quod *said.*
quoniam *what's-its-name.*

radde *read.*
rafte *bereft, robbed, took away.*
ragerie *hot passion, wantonness.*
rake-stele *rake-handle.*
raunson *ransom, payment.*
recche *heed, care.*
red(de) *read, (has read).*
redeth *comprehend, understand.*
redresse *redress, put right.*
reed *red.*
reedeth *read(s), study (studies).*
refreshed *refreshed.*
rekketh *concerns, troubles, cares.*
remembreth *remembers.*
remenant *remainder, rest.*
renne(th) *run(s).*
renomee *renown, fame.*
rente *tore out, ripped.*
repair *resort.*
repreeve *reprove, reproach.*
repreve *reproach, shame.*
requere *require of, demand.*
resonable *reasonable, sensible.*
revelour *reveller, rake.*
rewe (by) *one in a row, all along the row (*l.506*).*
reyn *rain.*
reysed *raised.*
richesse *wealth and noble rank.*
right *exactly, just.*
riot *riotousness.*
Romain *Roman.*
roode beem *beam which supports a cross.*
roos *rose.*
roule *roll, gad about.*
rowne *whisper.*
rubriche *rubric, canon, instruction.*
rude *low-born, vulgar.*
rym *rhyme, poetry.*
salwes *twigs, willow branches.*
sapience *wisdom.*
sauf(ly) *safe(ly).*
saugh *saw.*
savacioun *salvation.*
save *except.*
savoure *savour, taste.*
sawe *saying.*
say *saw.*
sayde *endeavoured, tried.*

science *knowledge, learning.*
seche *seek.*
secree *secret, trusty, discreet.*
seel *seal.*
seist *say (sayest).*
seistow *say you (sayest thou).*
seke *seek, search for.*
selde *seldom.*
selven *selves.*
sely *simple, innocent.*
senge *singe.*
sentence *meaning, opinion, subject.*
sepulcre *sepulchre, tomb.*
serchen *visit haunt.*
seten *sat.*
sette *supposed, reckoned, counted.*
seyden *said.*
seydest *said.*
seye *say, speak, see, perceive.*
seyn *say.*
shame *shy, ashamed.*
shap *shape, body.*
shapen *shaped, devised, fashioned, contrived.*
shende *harm, destroy.*
sheres *shears.*
sherte *shirt.*
shette *shut.*
shewe *show, reveal.*
shifte *provide, distribute.*
shipnes *stables, sheds.*
sho(o) *shoe.*
shorte *shorten.*
shrewe sb. *scoundrel, wretch,* **vb.** *beshrew, curse.*
shrewed *wicked.*
shrewednesse *cussedness, wickedness.*
shul *ought to, shall, must.*
side *body.*
sik *sickness, illness.*
siker *certain, for sure.*
siketh *sighs.*
singeth *sings.*
sith *since.*
sleighte *sleight, skill, craft, cunning.*
slik *sleek.*
smal *small.*
smale *slender.*
smok *smock.*
smoot *smote, struck.*
sodeynly *suddenly.*
soffre *suffer, endure.*
sojourne *linger, delay.*
solempnitee *solemnity, ceremony.*
som time *at sometime, once.*
someres *summer's.*
somme *some.*
somonour *summoner.*
sondry *sundry, various.*
song(en) *sang.*
sonne-beem *sunbeam.*
soore *sorely, badly.*
sooth *in truth, truly.*
sorwe *sorrow, grief.*
sory *sorrowful, sad.*
sothe *in truth, truly.*
soun *sound.*
soutiltee *subtlety.*
soverainetee *sovereignty, supremacy.*
spak *spoke.*
spareth *spare, cease, refrain.*
spaynel *spaniel.*
specially *specially, particularly concerned with.*
spectacle *eye-glass.*
spek *speak, say.*
spekestow *do you say (speakest thou).*
spille *spill, destroy, kill.*
split *destroyed, lost.*
spinning *spinning (yarns).*
spitously *spitefully.*
spyen *spy on.*
squiereth *escorts, accompanies.*
stable *stable, reliable, constant.*
statut *statute, law.*
sterte *start, leap, more quickly.*
sterven *starve, die (of hunger).*
stibourn *stubborn.*
stifly *strongly, boldly.*
stille *still, silent.*

stinte *ceased, left off.*
stirte *started, leapt up.*
stonde *stand, affirm.*
stoor *store, stock, value.*
stoundes *times, seasons.*
strange *foreign, external.*
sturdy *sturdy, energetic, vigorous.*
subtilly *subtly, cleverly, carefully.*
suffisant *adequate, satisfactory.*
suffiseth *suffices, satisfies.*
suffrable *patient, long-suffering.*
suffre *suffer, allow.*
suffreth *suffers, endures.*
suppose *suppose, guess.*
suretee *security.*
suspecioun *suspicion.*
suster *sister.*
swal *swelled.*
swere *swear.*
swich *such.*
swinke *labour, toil.*
swogh *swoon.*
swoor *swore.*
swyn *swine.*

taak *take.*
taken *accepted.*
talis *tales.*
Taur *Taurus.*
teche *teach, instruct.*
temporel *temporal, worldly.*
terme *term, duration.*
testament *will and testament.*
thanne *thin.*
thar *it is necessary.*
that *who.*
thee *thrive, prosper.*
thenketh *think, consider.*
thenne *thence.*
ther *wherever.*
ther as *wherever.*
therbifoore *before.*
therto, therwithal *in addition.*
thikke *thick.*
thilke *that same.*
thise *these.*
tho *those; then.*
thogh *though.*
thonder *thunder.*
thonder-dint *thunder-clap.*
thoughte *seemed.*
thow *thou*
thral *thrall, slave.*
thrifty *profitable, serviceable; respectable.*
thropes *thorpes, villages.*
thurgh *through.*
tikled *tickled, gave pleasure to.*
tikleth *tickles (the fancy), excites.*
tobroke *broken.*
tolde *reckoned, accounted.*
to-morn *tomorrow.*
tomorwe *tomorrow.*
tonge *tongue.*
tonne *tun, barrel.*
took *seized, hit.*
toold *told, disclosed.*
toolth *taste.*
tormentrie *torment, torture.*
touche *touch.*
toures *towers.*
tourne *turn.*
tow *tow, flax, hemp.*
to-yeere *this year.*
tree *tree, wood.*
treson *treason, betrayal.*
tresoor *treasure, wealth.*
trewely *truly.*
tribulacioun *tribulation.*
trouthe *troth, word, pledge.*
trowe *believe, think.*
trusteth *trust, believe in.*
tweye *two.*
twiste *twisted, tortured, tormented*

undermeles *afternoons.*
undertake *undertake, declare, warrant.*
unnethe(s) *hardly, scarcely at all.*
unreste *unrest, unease.*
unright *injury, wrong.*
up and down *in every way.*
upright *stretched out, at full length.*
usage *custom.*

usinge *accustomed to.*

vacacioun *rest from work.*
venerien *subject of (influenced by) Venus.*
verraily *truly.*
verray *true, real.*
vertu *virtue, power, force.*
vice *fault, defect; wickedness.*
vicious *bad, wicked.*
vigilies *vigils, meetings, or services on the eve of a festival.*
vileynie *rudeness, discourtesy, wrong, shameful deed.*
vileyns *rude, sinful.*
vinolent *full of wine, tipsy.*
visage *face.*
visitacioun *visit.*
vois *voice.*

walweth *wallows, tosses and turns.*
warde-cors *guardian, bodyguard.*
wardeyn *guardian.*
ware *wares, goods.*
wast *waste.*
wax *wax, grow, increase, become.*
wedde *wed, marry.*
weel *well, many, much; (used emphatically, fully completely).*
weilawey *alas, woe is me.*
weive *refrain from, forsake.*
welde *wield, manage, control.*
welked *withered.*
welle *well, source.*
wench *wench, woman.*
wende *thought, imagined.*
wene *suppose, imagine.*
wenestow *do you suppose (wenest thou).*
wered *wore.*
wereth *wears.*
werne *refuse, deny, forbid.*
werre *war, strife.*
wexe *wax, grow, increase.*
whan *when.*
what *why.*
wheither *whether, whichever.*
wher *where.*
whichthat *whom.*
whine *whinny.*
widwe *widow.*
wight *person.*
wilde *wild, violent.*
wilful *willing.*
winde *turn, toss about.*
winne *win, gain, get profit.*
winning *winning, profiting.*
wirche *work, act, perform.*
wirking *working, influence.*
wisdam *wisdom.*
wise *way, fashion, manner.*
wisse *instruct, teach, tell.*
wiste *knew.*
wit *wit, mind, reason, understanding, knowledge.*
wite *blame.*
withal *also, as well.*
witing *knowing, knowledge.*
wo *woe, unhappiness, misery.*
wode *wood.*
wol(e) *will, want, desire.*
wolde *wished to.*
woldest *would like to.*
wolt vb. *will.*
woltow *would you (wouldst thou).*
wont *was accustomed.*
wood *mad, angry.*
woot *know, discover.*
wormes *worms, maggots.*
worthy *worthy, respectable.*
wostow *do you know (wost thou).*
wreke *avenged.*
writ *writes.*
wroghte *wrought, created, made.*
wrong *wrung, punched, squeezed.*
wroot *wrote.*
wrothe *angry.*
wy *why.*
wyf *wife, woman.*
wyfhod *wifehood.*
wys *way, manner.*

yaf *gave.*
ybroght *brought.*

yds *done.*
yeer *year.*
yelden *yield up, surrender.*
yen *eyes.*
yeve *give.*
yeve up *give up, surrender.*
yeven *given.*
yerne *earnestly, eagerly, quickly.*
yflatered *flattered.*
ygrave *buried.*
yif *give.*
yifte *gift.*
yit *yet.*
yive *given.*
ylimed *caught, ensnared.*
ynogh *enough.*
yowthe *youth.*
yplesed *pleased.*
yrekened *reckoned.*
ysowe *sowed.*
ystint *ceased, left off, at an end.*
ywis *certainly, truly.*
ywroght *wrought, created, made.*

NOTES

NOTES

NOTES

NOTES

Pan study aids Titles published in the Brodie's Notes series

W. H. Auden Selected Poetry

Jane Austen Emma Mansfield Park Northanger Abbey Persuasion Pride and Prejudice Sense and Sensibility

Anthologies of Poetry Ten Twentieth Century Poets The Poet's Tale The Metaphysical Poets

Samuel Beckett Waiting for Godot

Arnold Bennett The Old Wives' Tale

William Blake Songs of Innocence and Experience

Robert Bolt A Man for All Seasons

Harold Brighouse Hobson's Choice

Charlotte Brontë Jane Eyre

Emily Brontë Wuthering Heights

Robert Browning Selected Poetry

John Bunyan The Pilgrim's Progress

Geoffrey Chaucer (parallel texts editions) The Franklin's Tale The Knight's Tale The Miller's Tale The Nun's Priest's Tale The Pardoner's Tale Prologue to the Canterbury Tales The Wife of Bath's Tale

Richard Church Over the Bridge

John Clare Selected Poetry and Prose

Samuel Taylor Coleridge Selected Poetry and Prose

Wilkie Collins The Woman in White

William Congreve The Way of the World

Joseph Conrad The Nigger of the Narcissus & Youth The Secret Agent Heart of Darkness

Charles Dickens Bleak House David Copperfield Dombey and Son Great Expectations Hard Times Little Dorrit Oliver Twist Our Mutual Friend A Tale of Two Cities

Gerald Durrell My Family and Other Animals

George Eliot Middlemarch The Mill on the Floss Silas Marner

T. S. Eliot Murder in the Cathedral Selected Poems

J. G. Farrell The Siege of Krishnapur

Henry Fielding Joseph Andrews

F. Scott Fitzgerald The Great Gatsby

E. M. Forster Howards End A Passage to India
Where Angels Fear to Tread

William Golding Lord of the Flies The Spire

Oliver Goldsmith Two Plays of Goldsmith: She Stoops to Conquer; The Good Natured Man

Graham Greene Brighton Rock The Power and the Glory
The Quiet American The Human Factor

Thom Gunn and Ted Hughes Selected Poems

Thomas Hardy Chosen Poems of Thomas Hardy
Far from the Madding Crowd Jude the Obscure
The Mayor of Casterbridge Return of the Native
Tess of the d'Urbervilles The Trumpet-Major The Woodlanders

L. P. Hartley The Go-Between The Shimp and the Anemone

Joseph Heller Catch-22

Ernest Hemingway For Whom the Bell Tolls
The Old Man and the Sea

Barry Hines A Kestrel for a Knave

Gerard Manley Hopkins Poetry and Prose of Gerard Manley Hopkins

Aldous Huxley Brave New World

Henry James Washington Square

Ben Jonson The Alchemist Volpone

James Joyce A Portrait of the Artist as a Young Man Dubliners

John Keats Selected Poems and Letters of John Keats

Ken Kesey One Flew over the Cuckoo's Nest

Rudyard Kipling Kim

D. H. Lawrence The Rainbow Selected Tales Sons and Lovers

Harper Lee To Kill a Mockingbird

Laurie Lee As I Walked out One Midsummer Morning
Cider with Rosie

Thomas Mann Death in Venice & Tonio Kröger

Christopher Marlowe Doctor Faustus Edward the Second

W. Somerset Maugham Of Human Bondage

Gavin Maxwell Ring of Bright Water

Thomas Middleton The Changeling

Arthur Miller The Crucible Death of a Salesman

John Milton A Choice of Milton's Verse Comus and Samson Agonistes Paradise Lost I, II

Sean O'Casey Juno and the Paycock
The Shadow of a Gunman and the Plough and the Stars

George Orwell Animal Farm 1984

John Osborne Luther

Alexander Pope Selected Poetry

J. B. Priestley An Inspector Calls

Siegfried Sassoon Memoirs of a Fox-Hunting Man

Peter Shaffer The Royal Hunt of the Sun

William Shakespeare Antony and Cleopatra As You Like It Coriolanus Hamlet Henry IV (Part I) Henry IV (Part II) Henry V Julius Caesar King Lear Love's Labour's Lost Macbeth Measure for Measure The Merchant of Venice A Midsummer Night's Dream Much Ado about Nothing Othello Richard II Richard III Romeo and Juliet The Sonnets The Taming of the Shrew The Tempest Twelfth Night The Winter's Tale

G. B. Shaw Arms and the Man
Caesar and Cleopatra The Doctor's Dilemma Pygmalion Saint Joan

Richard Sheridan Plays of Sheridan: The Rivals; The Critic; The School for Scandal

John Steinbeck The Grapes of Wrath Of Mice and Men & The Pearl

Tom Stoppard Rosencrantz and Guildenstern are Dead

J. M. Synge The Playboy of the Western World

Jonathan Swift Gulliver's Travels

Alfred Tennyson Selected Poetry

William Thackeray Vanity Fair

Flora Thompson Lark Rise to Candleford

Dylan Thomas Under Milk Wood

Anthony Trollope Barchester Towers

Mark Twain Huckleberry Finn

Keith Waterhouse Billy Liar

Evelyn Waugh Decline and Fall Scoop

H. G. Wells The History of Mr Polly The War of the Worlds

John Webster The Duchess of Malfi The White Devil

Oscar Wilde The Importance of Being Earnest

Virginia Woolf To the Lighthouse

William Wordsworth The Prelude (Books 1, 2)

William Wycherley The Country Wife

John Wyndham The Chrysalids

W. B. Yeats Selected Poetry

Pan study aids

Published jointly by Heinemann Educational Books and Pan Books

Pan Study Aids is a major new series developed to help school and college students prepare for examinations. All the authors are experienced teachers/examiners at O level, School Certificate and equivalent examinations and authors of textbooks used in schools and colleges worldwide

Each volume in the series:

- explains its subject and covers clearly and concisely and with excellent illustrations the essential points of the syllabus, drawing attention to common areas of difficulty and to areas which carry most marks in the exam
- gives guidance on how to plan revision, and prepare for the exam, outlining what examiners are looking for
- provides practice by including typical exam questions and exercises

Titles available: Physics, Chemistry, Maths, Human Biology, English Language, Geography 1 & 2, Economics, Commerce, Accounts and Book-keeping, British Government and Politics, History 1 & 2, Effective Study Skills, French, German, Spanish, Sociology

Pan Literature Guides

Marguerite Alexander
An Introduction to Shakespeare and his Contemporaries
From the mid-sixteenth century to the closing of the theatres in 1642, English drama proved the finest flowering of the English renaissance. Marguerite Alexander's *Literature Guide* examines the themes and development of Elizabethan and Jacobean drama, going on to explore the social conditions and literary and folk traditions that combined to produce the period's unique poetry and drama.

John Cargill Thompson
An Introduction to British Drama 1660–1900
John Cargill Thompson's Literature Guide pinpoints fifty major landmarks of dramatic writing from the reopening of the theatres under the Stuart kings, the Restoration plays, through the sophisticated entertainments of Goldsmith and Sheridan, to the stages of Victorian England where Wilde and Pinero saw the curtain fall on the last act of the nineteenth century.

Benedict Nightingale
An Introduction to Fifty Modern British Plays
The last eighty years have seen a constant flow of fine theatre across the English-speaking stage – from the Edwardian finale of Shaw and Maugham, through the *entr'acte* of Coward and Priestley, to the new vision of the 1950s and the radical creativity of the last decade. Benedict Nightingale takes fifty important and influential plays, examining each in the context of the wider output of the playwright, and providing a lively and comprehensive survey of the drama of our times.